CHOCOLATE
FANTASIES

CHOCOLATE
FANTASIES

70 IRRESISTIBLE RECIPES TO DIE FOR

Christine France

HERMES
HOUSE

First published in 1998 by Hermes House

© Anness Publishing Limited 1998

Hermes House is an imprint of Anness Publishing Limited
Hermes House, 88–89 Blackfriars Road, London SE1 8HA

This edition published 1998 in the Necessities™ imprint by
The Warehouse Ltd., 26 The Warehouse Way, Northcote, Auckland, New Zealand

ISBN 1-84038-180-9

A CIP catalogue record for this book is available from the British Library

Publisher: Joanna Lorenz
Project Editors: Joanne Rippin, Linda Doeser
Assistant Editor: Emma Gray
Designers: Nigel Partridge, Siân Keogh
Special Photography: Don Last

Front cover: Lisa Tai, Designer; Thomas Odulate, Photographer;
Helen Trent, Stylist; Lucy McKelvie, Home Economist

Previously published as part of a larger compendium: *The Ultimate Encyclopedia of Chocolate*

Printed in Hong Kong/China

10 9 8 7 6 5 4 3 2 1

The authors and publishers would like to thank the following people for supplying
additional recipes in the book: Catherine Atkinson, Alex Barker, Carla Capalbo,
Maxine Clark, Frances Cleary, Carole Clements, Roz Denny, Nicola Diggins,
Joanne Farrow, Silvana Franco, Sarah Gates, Shirley Gill, Patricia Lousada,
Norma MacMillan, Sue Maggs, Sarah Maxwell, Janice Murfitt, Annie Nichols,
Angela Nilsen, Louise Pickford, Katherine Richmond, Hilaire Walden, Laura
Washburn, Steven Wheeler, Judy Williams, Elizabeth Wolf-Cohen.

Additional recipe photographs supplied by: Karl Adamson, Edward Allwright,
David Armstrong, Steve Baxter, James Duncan, Michelle Garrett,
Amanda Heywood, Tim Hill, David Jordan.

NOTES
For all recipes, quantities are given in both metric and imperial measures and,
where appropriate, measures are given in standard cups and spoons. Follow one
set, but not a mixture, because they are not interchangeable.

Standard spoon and cup measurements are level.
1 tsp = 5ml, 1 tbsp = 15ml; 1 cup = 250ml/8fl oz

Australian standard tablespoons are 20ml. Australian readers should use 3 tsp in
place of 1 tbsp for measuring small quantities of gelatine, cornflour, salt etc.

Medium eggs should be used unless otherwise stated.

CONTENTS

INTRODUCTION

Few people can resist it – whether a sumptuous and self-indulgent chocolate gâteau, a plate of melt-in-the-mouth profiteroles, a richly coated sundae or a decorative box of truffles. This book is packed with wickedly tempting recipes for those with a sweet tooth, chocolate-lovers and self-admitted, outright "chocoholics".

The book is divided into six chapters, with over 70 recipes for preparing superb confections with dark, milk and white chocolate. Cakes & Gâteaux ranges from morning coffee and afternoon tea-time treats, such as Chocolate Coconut Roulade and Frosted Chocolate Fudge, to magnificent dinner party centrepieces, such as Chocolate Redcurrant Torte and Meringue Gâteau with Chocolate Mascarpone. Hot Desserts includes such magical delights as Chocolate Crêpes with Plums and Port and Dark Chocolate Ravioli with White Chocolate and Cream Cheese Filling. Tarts, Pies & Cheesecakes boasts such favourites as Chocolate Tiramisu Tart and Mississippi Mud Pie, while Cold Desserts tantalizes the tastebuds with a selection of sorbets and ice creams. Anything from Little Cakes, Biscuits & Bars will bring the children running, while Sweets & Truffles offers more sophisticated pleasures, such as Double Chocolate-dipped Fruit, Rich Chocolate Pistachio Fudge and Cognac and Ginger Creams.

There is hardly a country in the western world that does not have chocolate as part of its culinary culture, whether it be a moist chocolate brownie from the United States, a chocolate-covered pancake from Hungary or an elegant French pastry. Indulge yourself on a chocolate-lover's dream journey – your only problem will be what to choose next!

TECHNIQUES

MELTING CHOCOLATE

If chocolate is being melted on its own, all the equipment must be completely dry, as water may cause the chocolate to thicken and become a stiff paste. For this reason, do not cover chocolate during or after melting it, as condensation could form. If chocolate does thicken, add a little pure white vegetable fat (not butter or margarine) and mix well. If this does not work, start again. Do not discard the thickened chocolate; melt it with cream to make a sauce.

With or without liquid, chocolate should be melted very slowly. It is easily burned or scorched, and then develops a bad flavour. If any steam gets into the chocolate, it can turn into a solid mass. If this happens, stir in a little pure white vegetable fat. Dark chocolate should not be heated above 50°C/120°F. Milk and white chocolate should not be heated above 45°C/110°F. Take particular care when melting white chocolate, which clogs very easily when subjected to heat.

MELTING CHOCOLATE OVER SIMMERING WATER

1 Chop or cut the chocolate into small pieces with a sharp knife to enable it to melt quickly and evenly.

2 Put the chocolate in the top of a double boiler or in a heatproof bowl over a saucepan of barely simmering water. The bowl should not touch the water.

3 Heat gently until the chocolate is melted and smooth, stirring occasionally. Remove from the heat and stir.

MELTING CHOCOLATE OVER DIRECT HEAT

When a recipe recommends melting chocolate with a liquid such as milk, cream or even butter, this can be done over direct heat in a saucepan.

1 Choose a heavy-based saucepan. Add the chocolate and liquid and melt over a low heat, stirring frequently, until the chocolate is melted and the mixture is smooth. Remove from heat immediately. This method is also used for making sauces, icings and some sweets.

2 Chocolate can also be melted in a very low oven. Preheat oven to 110°C/ 225°F/Gas ¼. Put the chocolate in an ovenproof bowl and place in the oven for a few minutes. Remove the chocolate before it is completely melted and stir until smooth.

MELTING CHOCOLATE IN THE MICROWAVE

Check the chocolate at frequent intervals during the cooking time. These times are for a 650–700 W oven and are approximate, as microwave ovens vary.

1 Place 115g/4oz chopped or broken dark, bittersweet or semi-sweet chocolate in a microwave-safe bowl and microwave on Medium for about 2 minutes. The same quantity of milk or white chocolate should be melted on Low for about 2 minutes.

2 Check the chocolate frequently during the cooking time. The chocolate will not change shape, but will start to look shiny. It must then be removed from the microwave and stirred until completely melted and smooth.

TEMPERING CHOCOLATE

TEMPERING CHOCOLATE

Tempering is the process of gently heating and cooling chocolate to stabilize the emulsification of cocoa solids and butterfat. This technique is generally used by professionals handling couverture chocolate. It allows the chocolate to shrink quickly (to allow easy release from a mould, for example with Easter eggs) or to be kept at room temperature for several weeks or months without losing its crispness and shiny surface. All solid chocolate is tempered in production, but once melted loses its "temper" and must be tempered again unless it is to be used immediately. Untempered chocolate tends to "bloom" or becomes dull and streaky or takes on a cloudy appearance. This can be avoided if the melted chocolate is put in the fridge immediately: chilling the chocolate solidifies the cocoa butter and prevents it from rising to the surface and "blooming". General baking and dessert-making do not require tempering, which is a fussy procedure and takes practice. However, it is useful to be aware of the technique when preparing sophisticated decorations, moulded chocolates or coatings. Most shapes can be made without tempering if they are chilled immediately.

EQUIPMENT

To temper chocolate successfully, you will need a marble slab or similar cool, smooth surface, such as an upturned baking sheet. A flexible plastic scraper is ideal for spreading the chocolate, but you can use a palette knife. As the temperature is crucial, you will need a chocolate thermometer. Look for this at a specialist kitchen supply shop, where you may also find blocks of tempered chocolate, ready for immediate use.

__1__ Break up the chocolate into small pieces and place it in the top of a double boiler or a heatproof bowl over a saucepan of hot water. Heat gently until just melted.

__2__ Remove from the heat. Spoon about three-quarters of the melted chocolate on to a marble slab or other cool, smooth, non-porous work surface.

__3__ With a flexible plastic scraper or palette knife, spread the chocolate thinly, then scoop it up before spreading it again. Repeat the sequence, keeping the chocolate constantly on the move, for about 5 minutes.

__4__ Using a chocolate thermometer, check the temperature of the chocolate as you work it. As soon as the temperature registers 28°C/82°F, tip the chocolate back into the bowl and stir into the remaining chocolate.

__5__ With the addition of the hot chocolate, the temperature should now be 32°C/90°F, making the chocolate ready for use. To test, drop a little of the chocolate from a spoon on to the marble; it should set very quickly.

STORING CHOCOLATE

Chocolate can be stored successfully for up to a year if the conditions are favourable. This means a dry place with a temperature of around 20°C/68°F. At higher temperatures, the chocolate may develop white streaks as the fat comes to the surface. Although this will not spoil the flavour, it will mar the appearance of the chocolate, making it unsuitable for use as a decoration. When storing chocolate, keep it cool and dry. Place inside an airtight container, away from strong smelling foods. Check the "best before" dates on the pack.

Piping with Chocolate

Pipe chocolate directly on to a cake, or on to non-stick baking paper to make run-outs, small outlined shapes or irregular designs. After melting the chocolate, allow it to cool slightly so it just coats the back of a spoon. If it still flows freely it will be too runny to hold its shape when piped. When it is the right consistency, you then need to work fast as the chocolate will set quickly. Use a paper piping bag and keep the pressure very tight, as the chocolate will flow readily without encouragement.

Making a Paper Piping Bag

A non-stick paper cone is ideal for piping small amounts of messy liquids like chocolate as it is small, easy to handle and disposable, unlike a conventional piping bag, which will need cleaning.

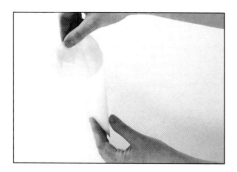

1 Fold a square of non-stick baking paper in half to form a triangle. With the triangle point facing you, fold the left corner down to the centre.

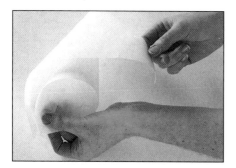

2 Fold the right corner down and wrap it around the folded left corner to form a cone. Fold the ends into the cone.

3 Spoon the melted chocolate into the cone and fold the top edges over. When ready to pipe, snip off the end of the point neatly to make a tiny hole, about 3 mm/⅛ in in diameter.

4 Another method is to use a small heavy-duty freezer or plastic bag. Place a piping nozzle in one corner of the bag, so that it is in the correct position for piping. Fill as above, squeezing the filling into one corner and twisting the top to seal. Snip off the corner of the bag, if necessary, so that the tip of the nozzle emerges, and squeeze gently to pipe the design.

Chocolate Drizzles

You can have great fun making random shapes or, with a steady hand, special designs that will look great on cakes or biscuits.

1 Melt the chocolate and pour it into a paper cone or small piping bag fitted with a very small plain nozzle. Drizzle the chocolate on to a baking sheet lined with non-stick baking paper to make small, self-contained lattice shapes, such as circles or squares. Allow to set for 30 minutes then peel off the paper.

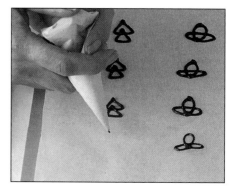

2 Chocolate can be used in many designs, such as flowers or butterflies. Use non-stick baking paper as tracing paper and pipe the chocolate over the chosen design or decorative shape.

3 For butterflies, pipe chocolate on to individually cut squares and leave until just beginning to set. Use a long, thin box (such as an egg carton) and place the butterfly shape in the box or between the cups so it is bent in the centre, creating the butterfly shape. Chill until needed.

Piping on to Cakes

This looks effective on top of a cake iced with coffee glacé icing.

1 Melt 50g/2oz each of white and plain dark chocolate in separate bowls, and allow to cool slightly. Place the chocolates in separate paper piping bags. Cut a small piece off the pointed end of each bag in a straight line.

2 Hold each piping bag in turn above the surface of the cake and pipe the chocolates all over as shown in the picture. Alternatively, pipe a freehand design in one continuous curvy line, first with one bag of chocolate, then the other.

PIPING CURLS

Make lots of these curly shapes and store them in a cool place ready for using as cake decorations. Try piping the lines in contrasting colours of chocolate to vary the effect.

1 Melt 115g/4oz chocolate and allow to cool slightly. Cover a rolling pin with baking parchment and attach it with tape. Fill a paper piping bag with the chocolate and cut a small piece off the pointed end in a straight line.

2 Pipe lines of chocolate backwards and forwards over the baking parchment.

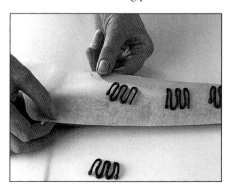

3 Leave the piped curls to set in a cool place, then carefully peel off the baking parchment. Use a palette knife to lift the curls on to the cake.

FEATHERING OR MARBLING CHOCOLATE

These two related techniques provide some of the easiest and most effective ways of decorating the top of a cake, and they are also used when making a swirled mixture for cut-outs. Chocolate sauce and double cream can also be feathered or marbled to decorate a dessert.

1 Melt two contrasting colours of chocolate and spread one over the cake or surface to be decorated.

2 Spoon the contrasting chocolate into a piping bag and pipe lines or swirls over the chocolate base.

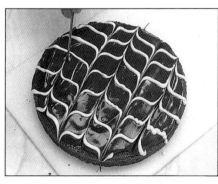

3 Working quickly before the chocolate sets, draw a skewer or cocktail stick through the swirls to create a feathered or marbled effect.

CHOCOLATE RUN-OUTS

Try piping the outline in one colour of chocolate and filling in the middle with another. The effect can be dramatic.

1 Tape a piece of greaseproof paper to a baking sheet or flat board. Draw around a shaped biscuit cutter on to the paper several times. Secure a piece of non-stick baking paper over the top.

2 Pipe over the outline of your design in a continuous thread.

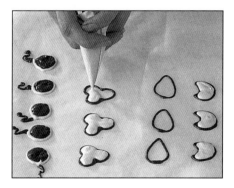

3 Cut the end off the other bag, making the hole slightly wider than before, and pipe the chocolate to fill in the outline so it looks slightly rounded. Leave the shapes to set in a cool place, then carefully lift them off the non-stick baking paper with a palette knife.

CAKES &
GATEAUX

FRENCH CHOCOLATE CAKE

SERVES 10

*250g / 9oz bittersweet chocolate, chopped into
small pieces
225g / 8oz / 1 cup unsalted butter, cut into
small pieces
90g / 3½oz / scant ½ cup granulated sugar
30ml / 2 tbsp brandy or orange-flavoured
liqueur
5 eggs
15ml / 1 tbsp plain flour
icing sugar, for dusting
whipped or soured cream, for serving*

1 Preheat oven to 180°C/350°F/Gas 4.
Generously grease a 23 x 5 cm/9 x 2 in
springform tin. Line the base with non-
stick baking paper and grease. Wrap the
bottom and sides of the tin in foil to
prevent water from seeping through into
the cake.

2 In a saucepan, over a low heat, melt the
chocolate, butter and sugar, stirring
frequently until smooth. Remove from
the heat, cool slightly and stir in the
brandy or liqueur.

3 In a large bowl beat the eggs lightly for
1 minute. Beat in the flour, then slowly
beat in the chocolate mixture until well
blended. Pour into the tin.

4 Place the springform tin in a large
roasting tin. Add enough boiling water to
come 2 cm/¾ in up the side of the
springform tin. Bake for 25–30 minutes,
until the edge of the cake is set but the
centre is still soft. Remove the
springform tin from the roasting tin and
remove the foil. Cool on a wire rack. The
cake will sink in the centre and become
its classic slim shape as it cools. Don't
worry if the surface cracks slightly.

5 Remove the side of the springform tin
and turn the cake on to a wire rack. Lift
off the springform tin base and then
carefully peel back the paper, so the base
of the cake is now the top. Leave the cake
on the rack until it is quite cold.

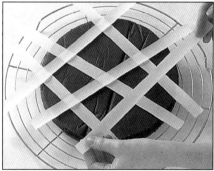

6 Cut 6–8 strips of non-stick baking
paper 2.5 cm/1 in wide and place
randomly over the cake. Dust the cake
with icing sugar, then carefully remove
the paper. Slide the cake on to a plate and
serve with whipped or soured cream.

MERINGUE GATEAU WITH CHOCOLATE MASCARPONE

SERVES ABOUT 10

4 egg whites
pinch of salt
175g/6oz/¾ cup caster sugar
5ml/1 tsp ground cinnamon
75g/3oz plain dark chocolate, grated
icing sugar and rose petals, to decorate

FOR THE FILLING

115g/4oz plain chocolate, chopped into
small pieces
5ml/1 tsp vanilla essence or rosewater
115g/4oz/½ cup mascarpone cheese

<u>1</u> Preheat oven to 150°C/300°F/Gas 2. Line two large baking sheets with non-stick baking paper. Whisk the egg whites with the salt in a clean, grease-free bowl until they form stiff peaks.
<u>2</u> Gradually whisk in half the sugar, then add the rest and whisk until the meringue is very stiff and glossy. Add the cinnamon and chocolate and whisk lightly to mix.

<u>3</u> Draw a 20 cm/8 in circle on the lining paper on one of the baking sheets, replace it upside down and spread the marked circle evenly with about half the meringue. Spoon the remaining meringue in 28–30 small neat heaps on both baking sheets. Bake for 1½ hours, until crisp.

<u>4</u> Make the filling. Melt the chocolate in a heatproof bowl over hot water. Cool slightly, then add the vanilla essence or rosewater and cheese. Cool the mixture until it holds it shape.

<u>5</u> Spoon the chocolate mixture into a large piping bag and sandwich the meringues together in pairs, reserving a small amount of filling for assembling the gâteau.
<u>6</u> Arrange the filled meringues on a serving platter, piling them up in a pyramid. Keep them in position with a few well-placed dabs of the reserved filling. Dust the pyramid with icing sugar, sprinkle with the rose petals and serve at once, while the meringues are crisp.

CHOCOLATE ALMOND MOUSSE CAKE

SERVES 8

*50g / 2oz plain dark chocolate, broken
into squares*
200g / 7oz marzipan, grated or chopped
200ml / 7fl oz / scant 1 cup milk
115g / 4oz / 1 cup self-raising flour
2 eggs, separated
*75g / 3oz / ½ cup light muscovado
sugar*

FOR THE MOUSSE FILLING

*115g / 4oz plain chocolate, chopped into
small pieces*
50g / 2oz / ¼ cup unsalted butter
2 eggs, separated
*30ml / 2 tbsp Amaretto di Saronno
liqueur*

FOR THE TOPPING

*1 quantity Chocolate Ganache
toasted flaked almonds, to decorate*

1 Preheat oven to 190°C/375°F/Gas 5.
Grease a deep 17 cm/6½ in square cake
tin and line with non-stick baking paper.
Combine the chocolate, marzipan and
milk in a saucepan and heat gently
without boiling, stirring until smooth.
2 Sift the flour into a bowl and add the
chocolate mixture and egg yolks, beating
until evenly mixed.

3 Whisk the egg whites in a clean, grease-
free bowl until stiff enough to hold firm
peaks. Whisk in the sugar gradually. Stir
about 15ml/1 tbsp of the whites into the
chocolate mixture to lighten it, then fold
in the rest.
4 Spoon the mixture into the tin,
spreading it evenly. Bake for 45–50
minutes, until well risen, firm and
springy to the touch. Leave to cool on a
wire rack.
5 Make the mousse filling. Melt the
chocolate with the butter in a small
saucepan over a low heat, then remove
from the heat and beat in the egg yolks
and Amaretto. Whisk the egg whites in a
clean, grease-free bowl until stiff, then
fold into the chocolate mixture.

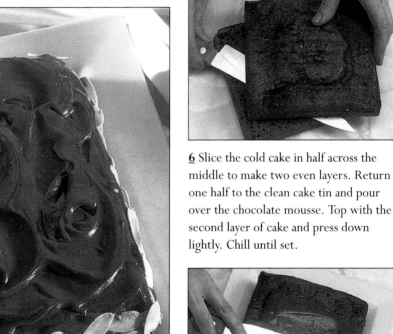

6 Slice the cold cake in half across the
middle to make two even layers. Return
one half to the clean cake tin and pour
over the chocolate mousse. Top with the
second layer of cake and press down
lightly. Chill until set.

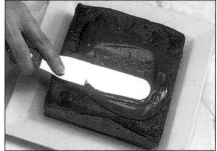

7 Turn the cake out on to a serving plate.
Allow the chocolate ganache to soften to
room temperature, then beat it to a soft,
spreading consistency. Spread the
chocolate ganache over the top and sides
of the cake, then press toasted flaked
almonds over the sides. Serve chilled.

SACHERTORTE

SERVES 10–12

225g / 8oz plain dark chocolate, chopped into
small pieces
150g / 5oz / ⅔ cup butter, softened
115g / 4oz / ½ cup caster sugar
8 eggs, separated
115g / 4oz / 1 cup plain flour
FOR THE GLAZE
225g / 8oz / scant 1 cup apricot jam
15ml / 1 tbsp lemon juice
FOR THE ICING
225g / 8oz plain dark chocolate, cut into
small pieces
200g / 7oz / scant 1 cup caster sugar
15ml / 1 tbsp golden syrup
250ml / 8fl oz / 1 cup double cream
5ml / 1 tsp vanilla essence
plain chocolate leaves, to decorate

5 Make the glaze. Heat the apricot jam with the lemon juice in a small saucepan until melted, then strain through a sieve into a bowl. Once the cake is cold, slice in half across the middle to make two even-size layers.

1 Preheat oven to 180°C / 350°F / Gas 4. Grease a 23 cm / 9 in round springform cake tin and line with non-stick baking paper. Melt the chocolate in a heatproof bowl over barely simmering water, then set the bowl aside.

2 Cream the butter with the sugar in a mixing bowl until pale and fluffy, then add the egg yolks, one at a time, beating after each addition. Beat in the melted chocolate, then sift the flour over the mixture and fold it in evenly.

3 Whisk the egg whites in a clean, grease-free bowl until stiff, then stir about a quarter of the whites into the chocolate mixture to lighten it. Fold in the remaining whites.

4 Tip the chocolate mixture into the prepared cake tin and smooth level. Bake for about 50–55 minutes or until firm. Cool in the tin for 5 minutes, then turn out carefully on to a wire rack and leave to cool completely.

6 Brush the top and sides of each layer with the apricot glaze, then sandwich them together. Place on a wire rack.

7 Make the icing. Mix the chocolate, sugar, golden syrup, cream and vanilla essence in a heavy saucepan. Heat gently, stirring constantly, until the mixture is thick and smooth. Simmer gently for 3–5 minutes, without stirring, until the mixture registers 95°C / 200°F on a sugar thermometer. Pour the icing quickly over the cake, spreading to cover the top and sides completely. Leave to set, decorate with chocolate leaves, then serve with whipped cream, if wished.

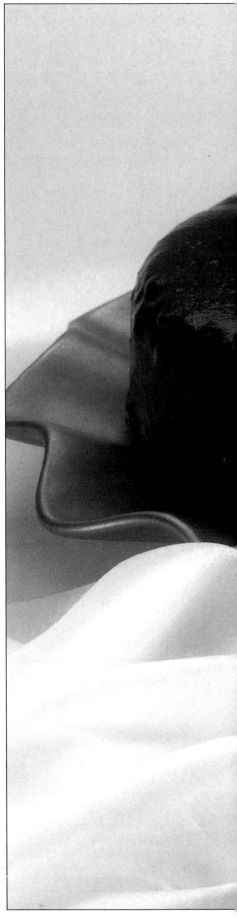

BLACK FOREST GATEAU

4 Prick each layer all over with a skewer or fork, then sprinkle with Kirsch. Using a hand-held electric mixer, whip the cream in a bowl until it starts to thicken, then gradually beat in the icing sugar and vanilla essence until the mixture begins to hold its shape.

5 To assemble, spread one cake layer with a thick layer of flavoured cream and top with about half the cherries. Spread a second cake layer with cream, top with the remaining cherries, then place it on top of the first layer. Top with the final cake layer.

6 Spread the remaining cream all over the cake. Dust a plate with icing sugar, and position the cake carefully in the centre. Press grated chocolate over the sides and decorate the cake with the chocolate curls and fresh or drained cherries.

SERVES 8–10

6 eggs
200g / 7oz / scant 1 cup caster sugar
5ml / 1 tsp vanilla essence
50g / 2oz / ½ cup plain flour
50g / 2oz / ½ cup cocoa powder
115g / 4oz / ½ cup unsalted butter, melted

FOR THE FILLING AND TOPPING
60ml / 4 tbsp Kirsch
600ml / 1 pint / 2½ cups double cream
30ml / 2 tbsp icing sugar
2.5ml / ½ tsp vanilla essence
675g / 1½lb jar stoned morello cherries,
well drained

TO DECORATE
icing sugar, for dusting
grated chocolate
Chocolate Curls
fresh or drained canned morello cherries

1 Preheat oven to 180°C / 350°F / Gas 4. Grease three 19 cm / 7½ in sandwich cake tins. Line the bottom of each with non-stick baking paper. Combine the eggs with the sugar and vanilla essence in a bowl and beat with a hand-held electric mixer until pale and very thick.

2 Sift the flour and cocoa powder over the mixture and fold in lightly and evenly with a metal spoon. Gently stir in the melted butter.

3 Divide the mixture among the prepared cake tins, smoothing them level. Bake for 15–18 minutes, until the cakes have risen and are springy to the touch. Leave them to cool in the tins for about 5 minutes, then turn out on to wire racks and leave to cool completely. Remove the lining paper from each cake layer.

CHOCOLATE GINGER CRUNCH CAKE

SERVES 6

150g/5oz plain chocolate, chopped into small pieces
50g/2oz/¼ cup unsalted butter
115g/4oz ginger nut biscuits
4 pieces of preserved stem ginger
30ml/2 tbsp stem ginger syrup
45ml/3 tbsp desiccated coconut

TO DECORATE

25g/1oz milk chocolate, chopped into small pieces
pieces of crystallized ginger

1 Grease a 15 cm/6 in flan ring and place it on a sheet of non-stick baking paper. Melt the plain chocolate with the butter in a heatproof bowl over barely simmering water. Remove from the heat and set aside.

2 Crush the biscuits into small pieces. Tip them into a bowl.

3 Chop the stem ginger fairly finely and mix with the crushed ginger nut biscuits.

4 Stir the biscuit mixture, ginger syrup and coconut into the melted chocolate and butter, mixing well until evenly combined.

5 Tip the mixture into the prepared flan ring and press down firmly and evenly. Chill in the fridge until set.

6 Remove the flan ring and slide the cake on to a plate. Melt the milk chocolate, drizzle it over the top and decorate with the pieces of crystallized ginger.

FROSTED CHOCOLATE FUDGE CAKE

SERVES 6–8

115g/4oz plain chocolate, chopped into small pieces
175g/6oz/¾ cup unsalted butter or margarine, softened
200g/7oz/generous 1 cup light muscovado sugar
5ml/1 tsp vanilla essence
3 eggs, beaten
150ml/¼ pint/⅔ cup Greek-style yogurt
150g/5oz/1¼ cups self-raising flour
icing sugar and chocolate curls, to decorate

FOR THE FROSTING

115g/4 oz plain dark chocolate, chopped into small pieces
50g/2oz/¼ cup unsalted butter
350g/12oz/2¼ cups icing sugar
90ml/6 tbsp Greek-style yogurt

1 Preheat oven to 190°C/375°F/Gas 5. Lightly grease two 20 cm/8 in round sandwich cake tins and line the base of each with non-stick baking paper. Melt the chocolate.

2 In a mixing bowl, cream the butter or margarine with the sugar until light and fluffy. Beat in the vanilla essence, then gradually add the beaten eggs, beating well after each addition.

3 Stir in the melted plain chocolate and yogurt evenly. Fold in the flour with a metal spoon.

4 Divide the mixture between the prepared tins. Bake for 25–30 minutes or until the cakes are firm to the touch. Turn out and cool on a wire rack.

5 Make the frosting. Melt the chocolate and butter in a saucepan over a low heat. Remove from the heat and stir in the icing sugar and yogurt. Mix with a rubber spatula until smooth, then beat until the frosting begins to cool and thicken slightly. Use about a third of the mixture to sandwich the cakes together.

6 Working quickly, spread the remainder over the top and sides. Sprinkle with icing sugar and decorate with chocolate curls.

CHOCOLATE BRANDY SNAP GATEAU

SERVES 8

225g/8oz plain dark chocolate, chopped
225g/8oz/1 cup unsalted butter, softened
200g/7oz/generous 1 cup dark
muscovado sugar
6 eggs, separated
5ml/1 tsp vanilla essence
150g/5oz/1¼ cups ground hazelnuts
60ml/4 tbsp fresh white breadcrumbs
finely grated rind of 1 large orange
1 quantity Chocolate Ganache, for filling
and frosting (omit jelly)
icing sugar, for dusting

FOR THE BRANDY SNAPS
50g/2oz/¼ cup unsalted butter
50g/2oz/¼ cup caster sugar
75g/3oz/⅓ cup golden syrup
50g/2oz/½ cup plain flour
5ml/1 tsp brandy

1 Preheat oven to 180°C/350°F/Gas 4. Grease two 20 cm/8 in sandwich cake tins and line the base of each with non-stick baking paper. Melt the chocolate and set aside to cool slightly.

2 Cream the butter with the sugar in a mixing bowl until pale and fluffy. Beat in the egg yolks and vanilla essence. Add the chocolate and mix thoroughly.

3 In a clean, grease-free bowl, whisk the egg whites to soft peaks, then fold them into the chocolate mixture with the ground hazelnuts, breadcrumbs and orange rind.

4 Divide the cake mixture between the prepared tins and smooth the tops. Bake for 25–30 minutes or until well risen and firm. Turn out on to wire racks. Leave the oven on.

5 Make the brandy snaps. Line two baking sheets with non-stick baking paper. Melt the butter, sugar and syrup together.

6 Stir the butter mixture until smooth. Remove from the heat and stir in the flour and brandy.

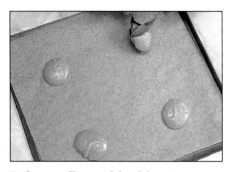

7 Place small spoonfuls of the mixture well apart on the baking sheets and bake for 8–10 minutes, until golden. Cool for a few seconds until firm enough to lift on to a wire rack.

8 Immediately pinch the edges of each brandy snap to create a frilled effect. If the biscuits become too firm, soften them briefly in the oven.

9 Sandwich the cake layers together with half the chocolate ganache, transfer to a plate and spread the remaining ganache on the top. Arrange the brandy snaps over the gâteau and dust with icing sugar.

COOK'S TIP
To save time, you could use ready-made brandy snaps. Simply warm them for a few minutes in the oven until they are pliable enough to shape. Or use as they are, filling them with cream, and arranging them so that they fan out from the centre of the gâteau.

CHOCOLATE COCONUT ROULADE

4 Scrape the mixture into the prepared tin, taking it right into the corners. Smooth the surface with a palette knife, then bake for 20–25 minutes or until well risen and springy to the touch.

5 Turn the cooked roulade out on to the sugar-dusted greaseproof paper and carefully peel off the lining paper. Cover with a damp, clean dish towel and leave to cool completely.

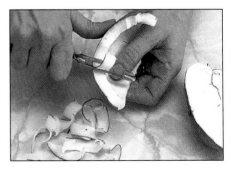

6 Make the filling. Whisk the cream with the whisky in a bowl until the mixture just holds it shape, grate the creamed coconut and stir in with the sugar.

SERVES 8

115g / 4oz / ½ cup caster sugar
5 eggs, separated
50g / 2oz / ½ cup cocoa powder

FOR THE FILLING

300ml / ½ pint / 1¼ cups double cream
45ml / 3 tbsp whisky
or brandy
50g / 2oz piece solid creamed
coconut
30ml / 2 tbsp caster sugar

FOR THE TOPPING

a piece of fresh coconut
dark chocolate for curls

1 Preheat oven to 180°C/350°F/Gas 4. Grease a 33 x 23 cm/13 x 9 in Swiss roll tin. Lay a large sheet of greaseproof paper or non-stick baking paper on the work surface and dust it evenly with 30ml/ 2 tbsp of the caster sugar.

2 Place the egg yolks in a heatproof bowl. Add the remaining caster sugar and whisk with a hand-held electric mixer until the mixture is thick enough to leave a trail. Sift the cocoa over, then fold in carefully and evenly with a metal spoon.

3 Whisk the egg whites in a clean, grease-free bowl until they form soft peaks. Fold about 15ml/1 tbsp of the whites into the chocolate mixture to lighten it, then fold in the rest evenly.

7 Uncover the sponge and spread about three-quarters of the cream mixture to the edges. Roll up carefully from a long side. Transfer to a plate, pipe or spoon the remaining cream mixture on top. Use a vegetable peeler to make coconut and chocolate curls and pile on the cake.

WHITE CHOCOLATE CAPPUCCINO GATEAU

SERVES 8

4 eggs
115g/4oz/½ cup caster sugar
15ml/1 tbsp strong black coffee
2.5ml/½ tsp vanilla essence
115g/4oz/1 cup plain flour
75g/3oz white chocolate, coarsely grated

FOR THE FILLING
120ml/4fl oz/½ cup double cream
15ml/1 tbsp coffee liqueur

FOR THE FROSTING AND TOPPING
15ml/1 tbsp coffee liqueur
1 quantity Chocolate Frosting, using white chocolate and 225g/8oz/2 cups icing sugar

white chocolate curls
cocoa powder or ground cinnamon,
for dusting

1 Preheat oven to 180°C/350°F/Gas 4. Grease two 18 cm/7 in round sandwich cake tins and line the base of each with non-stick baking paper.

2 Combine the eggs, caster sugar, coffee and vanilla essence in a large heatproof bowl. Place over a saucepan of hot water and whisk until pale and thick.

3 Sift half the flour over the mixture; fold in gently and evenly. Fold in the remaining flour with the grated white chocolate.

4 Divide the mixture between the prepared tins and smooth level. Bake for 20–25 minutes, until firm and golden brown, then turn out on wire racks and leave to cool completely.

5 Make the filling. Whip the cream with the coffee liqueur in a bowl until it holds its shape. Spread over one of the cakes, then place the second layer on top.

6 Stir the coffee liqueur into the frosting. Spread over the top and sides of the cake, swirling with a palette knife. Top with curls of white chocolate and dust with cocoa or cinnamon. Transfer the cake to a serving plate and set aside until the frosting has set. Serve the gâteau on the day it was made, if possible.

WHITE CHOCOLATE CELEBRATION CAKE

SERVES 40–50

900g / 2lb / 8 cups plain flour
2.5ml / ½ tsp salt
20ml / 4 tsp bicarbonate of soda
450g / 1lb white chocolate, chopped
475ml / 16fl oz / 2 cups whipping cream
450g / 1lb / 2 cups unsalted butter, softened
900g / 2lb / 4 cups caster sugar
12 eggs
20ml / 4 tsp lemon essence
grated rind of 2 lemons
335ml / 11fl oz / 1⅓ cups buttermilk
lemon curd, for filling
chocolate leaves, to decorate
FOR THE LEMON SYRUP
200g / 7oz / scant 1 cup granulated sugar
250ml / 8fl oz / 1 cup water
60ml / 4 tbsp lemon juice
FOR THE BUTTERCREAM
675g / 1½lb white chocolate chopped
1kg / 2¼lb cream cheese, softened
500g / 1¼lb / 2½ cups unsalted butter, at room temperature
60ml / 4 tbsp lemon juice
5ml / 1 tsp lemon essence

1 Divide all the ingredients into two equal batches, so that the quantities are more manageable. Use each batch to make one cake. Preheat oven to 180°C/350°F/Gas 4. Grease a 30 cm/ 12 in round cake tin. Base-line with non-stick baking paper. Sift the flour, salt and bicarbonate of soda into a bowl and set aside. Melt the chocolate and cream in a saucepan over a medium heat, stirring until smooth. Set aside to cool to room temperature.

VARIATION

For a summer celebration, decorate the cake with raspberries and white chocolate petals. To make the petals, you will need about 20 x 7.5 cm/3 in foil squares. Spread melted white chocolate thinly over each piece of foil, so that it resembles a rose petal. Before the chocolate sets, bend the foil up to emphasize the petal shape. When set, peel away the foil.

2 Beat the butter until creamy, then add the sugar and beat for 2–3 minutes. Beat in the eggs, then slowly beat in the melted chocolate, lemon essence and rind. Gradually add the flour mixture, alternately with the buttermilk, to make a smooth pouring mixture. Pour into the tin and bake for 1 hour or until a skewer inserted in the cake comes out clean.

3 Cool in the tin for 10 minutes, then invert the cake on a wire rack and cool completely. Wrap in clear film until ready to assemble. Using the second batch of ingredients, make another cake in the same way.

4 Make the lemon syrup. In a small saucepan, combine the sugar and water. Over a medium heat, bring to the boil, stirring until the sugar dissolves. Remove from the heat, stir in the lemon juice and cool completely. Store in an airtight container until required.

5 Make the buttercream. Melt the chocolate. Cool slightly. Beat the cream cheese in a bowl until smooth. Gradually beat in the cooled white chocolate, then the butter, lemon juice and essence. Chill.

6 Split each cake in half. Spoon syrup over each layer, let it soak in, then repeat. Spread the bottom half of each cake with lemon curd and replace the tops.

7 Gently beat the buttercream in a bowl until creamy. Spread a quarter over the top of one of the filled cakes. Place the second filled cake on top. Spread a small amount of softened butter over the top and sides of the cake to create a smooth, crumb-free surface. Chill for 15 minutes, so that the buttercream sets a little.

8 Place the cake on a serving plate. Set aside a quarter of the remaining buttercream for piping, then spread the rest evenly over the top and sides of the filled cake.

9 Spoon the reserved buttercream into a large icing bag fitted with a small star tip. Pipe a shell pattern around the rim of the cake. Decorate with chocolate leaves, made with dark or white chocolate (or a mixture) and fresh flowers.

RICH CHOCOLATE LEAF GATEAU

SERVES 8

*75g / 3oz plain dark chocolate, broken
into squares
150ml / ¼ pint / ⅔ cup milk
175g / 6oz / ¾ cup unsalted butter, softened
250g / 9oz / 1⅓ cups light muscovado sugar
3 eggs
250g / 9oz / 2¼ cups plain flour
10ml / 2 tsp baking powder
75ml / 5 tbsp single cream*
FOR THE FILLING AND TOPPING
*60ml / 4 tbsp raspberry conserve
1 quantity Chocolate Ganache
dark and white chocolate leaves*

1 Preheat oven to 190°C/375°F/Gas 5.
Grease and base-line two 22 cm/8½ in
sandwich cake tins. Melt the chocolate
with the milk over a low heat and allow
to cool slightly.

2 Cream the butter with the light
muscovado sugar in a mixing bowl until
light and fluffy. Add the eggs, one at a
time, beating well after each addition.
3 Sift the flour and baking powder over
the mixture and fold in gently but
thoroughly. Stir in the chocolate mixture
and the cream, mixing until smooth.
Divide between the prepared tins and
level the tops.

4 Bake the cakes for 30–35 minutes or
until they are well risen and firm to the
touch. Cool in the tins for a few minutes,
then turn out on to wire racks.

5 Sandwich the cake layers together with
the raspberry conserve. Spread the
chocolate ganache over the cake and
swirl with a knife. Place the cake on a
serving plate, then decorate with the
chocolate leaves.

CARIBBEAN CHOCOLATE RING WITH RUM SYRUP

SERVES 8–10

115g/4oz/½ cup unsalted butter
115g/4oz/¾ cup light muscovado sugar
2 eggs, beaten
2 ripe bananas, mashed
30ml/2 tbsp desiccated coconut
30ml/2 tbsp soured cream
115g/4oz/1 cup self-raising flour
45ml/3 tbsp cocoa powder
2.5ml/½ tsp bicarbonate of soda

FOR THE SYRUP
115g/4oz/½ cup caster sugar
30ml/2 tbsp dark rum
50g/2oz plain dark chocolate, chopped

TO DECORATE
mixture of tropical fruits, such as mango, pawpaw, starfruit and cape gooseberries
chocolate shapes or curls

1 Preheat oven to 180°C/350°F/Gas 4. Grease a 1.5 litre/2½ pint/6¼ cup ring tin with butter.

2 Cream the butter and sugar in a bowl until light and fluffy. Add the eggs gradually, beating well, then mix in the bananas, coconut and soured cream.

3 Sift the flour, cocoa and bicarbonate of soda over the mixture and fold in thoroughly and evenly.

4 Tip into the prepared tin and spread evenly. Bake for 45–50 minutes, until firm to the touch. Cool for 10 minutes in the tin, then turn out to finish cooling on a wire rack.

5 For the syrup, place the sugar in a small pan. Add 60ml/4 tbsp water and heat gently, stirring occasionally until dissolved. Bring to the boil and boil rapidly, without stirring, for 2 minutes. Remove from the heat.

6 Add the rum and chocolate to the syrup and stir until the mixture is melted and smooth, then spoon evenly over the top and sides of the cake.

7 Decorate the ring with tropical fruits and chocolate shapes or curls.

White Chocolate Mousse and Strawberry Layer Cake

4 Make the mousse filling. In a medium saucepan over a low heat, melt the chocolate and cream until smooth, stirring frequently. Stir in the rum or strawberry-flavoured liqueur and pour into a bowl. Chill until just set. With a wire whisk, whip lightly.

Serves 10

115g/4oz fine white chocolate, chopped into small pieces
120ml/4fl oz/½ cup double cream
120ml/4fl oz/½ cup milk
15ml/1 tbsp rum or vanilla essence
115g/4oz/½ cup unsalted butter, softened
175g/6oz/¾ cup granulated sugar
3 eggs
225g/8oz/2 cups plain flour
10ml/2 tsp baking powder
pinch of salt
675g/1½lb fresh strawberries, sliced, plus extra for decoration
750ml/1¼ pints/3 cups whipping cream
30ml/2 tbsp rum or strawberry-flavoured liqueur

White Chocolate Mousse Filling

250g/9oz white chocolate, chopped into small pieces
350ml/12fl oz/1½ cups double cream
30ml/2 tbsp rum or strawberry-flavoured liqueur

1 Preheat oven to 180°C/350°F/Gas 4. Grease and flour two 23 x 5 cm/9 x 2 in cake tins. Line the base of the tins with non-stick baking paper. Melt the chocolate and cream in a double boiler over a low heat, stirring until smooth. Stir in the milk and rum or vanilla essence, and set aside to cool.
2 In a large mixing bowl, beat the butter and sugar with a hand-held electric mixer for 3–5 minutes, until light and creamy, scraping the sides of the bowl occasionally. Add the eggs one at a time, beating well after each addition. In a small bowl, stir together the flour, baking powder and salt. Alternately add flour and melted chocolate to the egg mixture in batches, until just blended. Pour the mixture into the tins and spread evenly.
3 Bake for 20–25 minutes, until a skewer inserted in the cake comes out clean. Cool in the tin for 10 minutes, then turn cakes out on to a wire rack, peel off the paper and cool completely.

5 Assemble the cake. With a serrated knife, slice both cake layers in half, making four layers. Place one layer on the plate and spread one third of the mousse on top. Arrange one third of the sliced strawberries over the mousse. Place the second layer on top and spread with another third of the mousse. Arrange another third of the sliced strawberries over the mousse. Place the third layer on top and spread with the remaining mousse. Cover with the remaining sliced strawberries. Top with the last cake layer.
6 Whip the cream with the rum or liqueur until firm peaks form. Spread about half the whipped cream over the top and the sides of the cake. Spoon the remaining cream into a decorating bag fitted with a medium star tip and pipe scrolls on top of the cake. Decorate with the remaining sliced strawberries, pressing half of them into the cream on the side of the cake and arranging the rest on top.

CHOCOLATE CHESTNUT ROULADE

SERVES 10–12

*175g/6oz bittersweet chocolate, chopped into
small pieces*
30ml/2 tbsp cocoa powder, sifted
60ml/4 tbsp hot strong coffee or espresso
6 eggs, separated
75g/3oz/6 tbsp caster sugar
pinch of cream of tartar
5ml/1 tsp pure vanilla essence
cocoa powder, for dusting
glacé chestnuts, to decorate

CHESTNUT CREAM FILLING

475ml/16fl oz/2 cups double cream
30ml/2 tbsp rum or coffee-flavoured liqueur
*350g/12oz/1½ cups canned sweetened
chestnut purée*
115g/4oz bittersweet chocolate, grated

4 Dust a dish towel with cocoa. Turn the
cake out on to the towel immediately and
remove the paper. Trim off any crisp
edges. Starting at a narrow end, roll the
cake and towel together Swiss roll
fashion. Cool completely.

5 Make the filling. Whip the cream and
rum or liqueur until soft peaks form.
Beat a spoonful of cream into the
chestnut purée to lighten it, then fold in
the remaining cream and grated
chocolate. Set aside a quarter of this
mixture for the decoration. Unroll the
cake and spread chestnut cream to within
2.5 cm/1 in of the edge.

6 Using a dish towel to lift the cake,
carefully roll it up again. Place seam-
side down on a serving plate. Spread
some of the reserved chestnut cream
over the top and use the rest for
piped rosettes. Decorate with the
glacé chestnuts.

1 Preheat oven to 180°C/350°F/Gas 4.
Lightly grease the base and sides of a
39 x 27 x 2.5 cm/15½ x 10½ x 1 in Swiss
roll tin. Line with non-stick baking paper,
allowing a 2.5 cm/1 in overhang. Melt
the chocolate. Dissolve the cocoa in the
hot coffee to make a paste. Set aside.

2 Using a hand-held mixer, beat the egg
yolks with half the sugar in a mixing bowl
until pale and thick. Slowly beat in the
melted chocolate and cocoa-coffee paste
until just blended. In a separate bowl,
beat the egg whites and cream of tartar
until stiff peaks form. Sprinkle the
remaining sugar over the whites in two
batches and beat until the whites are
stiff and glossy, then beat in the
vanilla essence.

3 Stir a spoonful of the whites into the
chocolate mixture to lighten it, then
fold in the rest. Spoon into the tin.
Bake for 20–25 minutes or until the
cake springs back when touched with
a fingertip.

CHOCOLATE REDCURRANT TORTE

SERVES 8–10

115g / 4oz / ½ cup unsalted butter, softened
115g / 4oz / ⅔ cup dark muscovado sugar
2 eggs
150ml / ¼ pint / ⅔ cup soured cream
150g / 5oz / 1¼ cups self-raising flour
5ml / 1 tsp baking powder
50g / 2oz / ½ cup cocoa powder
75g / 3oz / ¾ cup stemmed redcurrants, plus
115g / 4oz / 1 cup redcurrant sprigs, to decorate

FOR THE ICING

150g / 5oz plain chocolate, chopped into small pieces
45ml / 3 tbsp redcurrant jelly
30ml / 2 tbsp dark rum
120ml / 4fl oz / ½ cup double cream

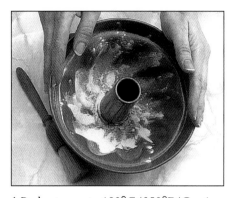

1 Preheat oven to 180°C/350°F/Gas 4. Grease a 1.2 litre/2 pint/5 cup ring tin and dust lightly with flour. Cream the butter with the sugar in a mixing bowl until pale and fluffy. Beat in the eggs and soured cream until thoroughly mixed.

2 Sift the flour, baking powder and cocoa over the mixture, then fold in lightly and evenly. Fold in the stemmed redcurrants. Spoon the mixture into the prepared tin and smooth the surface level. Bake for 40–50 minutes or until well risen and firm. Turn out on to a wire rack and leave to cool completely.

3 Make the icing. Mix the chocolate, redcurrant jelly and rum in a heatproof bowl. Set the bowl over simmering water and heat gently, stirring occasionally, until melted. Remove from the heat and cool to room temperature, then add the double cream, a little at a time. Mix well.

4 Transfer the cooked cake to a serving plate. Spoon the icing evenly over the cake, allowing it to drizzle down the sides. Decorate with redcurrant sprigs just before serving.

COOK'S TIP

Use a decorative gugelhupf tin or mould, if you have one. When preparing it, add a little cocoa powder to the flour used for dusting the greased tin, as this will prevent the cooked chocolate cake from being streaked with white.

CHOCOLATE BOX WITH CARAMEL MOUSSE AND BERRIES

SERVES 8–10

275g / 10oz plain chocolate, chopped into
small pieces

FOR THE CARAMEL MOUSSE

4 x 50g / 2oz chocolate-coated caramel bars,
coarsely chopped
25ml / 1½ tbsp milk or water
350ml / 12fl oz / 1½ cups double cream
1 egg white

FOR THE CARAMEL SHARDS

115g / 4oz / ½ cup granulated sugar
60ml / 4 tbsp water

FOR THE TOPPING

115g / 4oz fine quality white chocolate,
chopped into small pieces
350ml / 12fl oz / 1½ cups double cream
450g / 1lb mixed berries or cut up fruits such
as raspberries, strawberries, blackberries or
sliced nectarine and orange segments

1 Prepare the chocolate box. Turn a
23 cm / 9 in square baking tin bottom-
side up. Mould a piece of foil around the
tin, then turn it right side up and line it
with the foil, pressing against the edges to
make the foil as smooth as possible.

2 Place the plain chocolate in a heatproof
bowl over a saucepan of simmering water
Stir until the chocolate has melted and is
smooth. Immediately pour the melted
chocolate into the lined tin. Tilt to coat
the bottom and sides evenly, keeping the
top edges of the sides as straight as
possible. As the chocolate coats the sides,
tilt the pan again to coat the corners and
sides once more. Chill until firm.

3 Place the caramel bars and milk or
water in a heatproof bowl. Place over a
pan of simmering water and stir until
melted. Remove the bowl from the heat
and cool for 10 minutes, stirring
occasionally.

4 Using a hand-held electric mixer, whip
the cream in a bowl until soft peaks form.
Stir a spoonful of the whipped cream into
the caramel mixture to lighten it, then
fold in the remaining cream. In another
bowl beat the egg white until just stiff.
Fold the egg white into the mousse
mixture. Pour into the box. Chill for
several hours or overnight, until set.

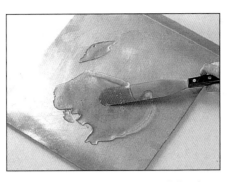

5 Meanwhile, make the caramel shards.
Lightly oil a baking sheet. In a small pan
over a low heat, dissolve the sugar in the
water, swirling the pan gently. Increase
the heat and boil the mixture for 4–5
minutes, until the sugar begins to turn a
pale golden colour. Protecting your hand
with an oven glove, immediately pour the
mixture on to the oiled sheet. Tilt the
sheet to distribute the caramel in an even
layer. (*Do not touch – caramel is dangerously
hot.*) Cool completely, then using a metal
palette knife, lift the caramel off the
baking sheet and break into pieces.

6 Make the topping. Combine the white
chocolate and 120ml / 4fl oz / ½ cup of the
cream in a small pan and melt over a low
heat until smooth, stirring frequently.
Strain into a medium bowl and cool to
room temperature, stirring occasionally.
In another bowl, beat the remaining
cream with a hand-held electric mixer,
until firm peaks form. Stir a spoonful of
cream into the white chocolate mixture,
then gently fold in the remaining
whipped cream.

7 Using the foil as a guide, remove the
mousse-filled box from the tin and peel
the foil carefully from the sides, then the
bottom. Slide the box gently on to a
serving plate.

8 Spoon the chocolate-cream mixture
into a piping bag fitted with a medium
star tip. Pipe a decorative design of
rosettes or shells over the surface of the
set mousse. Decorate the cream-topped
box with the mixed berries or cut up
fruits and the caramel shards.

HOT
DESSERTS

DARK CHOCOLATE RAVIOLI WITH WHITE CHOCOLATE AND CREAM CHEESE FILLING

SERVES 4

175g/6oz/1½ cups plain flour
25g/1oz/¼ cup cocoa powder
salt
30ml/2 tbsp icing sugar
2 large eggs, beaten
15ml/1tbsp olive oil
single cream and grated chocolate, to serve

FOR THE FILLING

175g/6oz white chocolate, chopped
350g/12oz/3 cups cream cheese
1 egg, plus 1 beaten egg to seal

1 Make the pasta. Sift the flour with the cocoa, salt and icing sugar on to a work surface. Make a well in the centre and pour the eggs and oil in. Mix together with your fingers. Knead until smooth. Alternatively, make the dough in a food processor, then knead by hand. Cover and rest for at least 30 minutes.

2 To make the filling, melt the white chocolate in a heatproof bowl placed over a pan of simmering water. Cool slightly. Beat the cream cheese in a bowl, then beat in the chocolate and eggs. Spoon into a piping bag fitted with a plain nozzle.

3 Cut the dough in half and wrap one portion in clear film. Roll the pasta out thinly to a rectangle on a lightly floured surface, or use a pasta machine. Cover with a clean damp dish towel and repeat with the remaining pasta.

4 Pipe small mounds (about 5ml/1 tsp) of filling in even rows, spacing them at 4 cm/1½ in intervals across one piece of the dough. Using a pastry brush, brush the spaces of dough between the mounds with beaten egg.

5 Using a rolling pin, lift the remaining sheet of pasta over the dough with the filling. Press down firmly between the pockets of filling, pushing out any trapped air. Cut the filled chocolate pasta into rounds with a serrated ravioli cutter or sharp knife. Transfer to a floured dish towel. Leave for 1 hour to dry out, ready for cooking.

6 Bring a frying pan of water to the boil and add the ravioli a few at a time, stirring to prevent them sticking together. (Adding a few drops of a bland oil to the water will help, too.) Simmer gently for 3–5 minutes, remove with a perforated spoon and serve with a generous splash of single cream and grated chocolate.

Chocolate Almond Meringue Pie

Serves 6

175g/6oz/1½ cups plain flour
50g/2oz/½ cup ground rice
150g/5oz/⅔ cup unsalted butter
finely grated rind of 1 orange
1 egg yolk
flaked almonds and melted plain dark
chocolate, to decorate

For the Filling

150g/5oz plain dark chocolate, chopped into
small pieces
50g/2oz/4 tbsp unsalted butter, softened
75g/3oz/6 tbsp caster sugar
10ml/2 tsp cornflour
4 egg yolks
75g/3oz/¾ cup ground almonds

For the Meringue

3 egg whites
150g/5oz/⅔ cup caster sugar

1 Sift the flour and ground rice into a bowl. Rub in the butter until the mixture resembles breadcrumbs. Stir in the orange rind. Add the egg yolks; bring the dough together. Roll out and use to line a 23 cm/9 in round flan tin. Chill.

2 Preheat oven to 190°C/375°F/Gas 5. Prick the pastry base, cover with grease-proof paper weighed down with baking beans and bake blind for 10 minutes.

3 Make the filling. Melt the chocolate, then cream the butter with the sugar in a bowl, and beat in the cornflour and egg yolks. Fold in the almonds, then the melted chocolate. Remove the paper and beans from the pastry case and add the filling. Bake for a further 10 minutes.

4 Make the meringue. Whisk the egg whites in a clean, grease-free bowl until stiff, then gradually whisk in about half the caster sugar. Fold in the remaining sugar with a metal spoon.

5 Spoon the meringue over the chocolate filling, lifting it up with the back of the spoon to form peaks. Reduce the oven temperature to 180°C/350°F/Gas 4 and bake the pie for 15–20 minutes or until the topping is pale gold. Serve warm, scattered with the almonds and drizzled with the melted chocolate.

MAGIC CHOCOLATE MUD PUDDING

SERVES 4

50g/2oz/4 tbsp butter, plus extra for greasing
90g/3½oz/scant 1 cup self-raising flour
5ml/1 tsp ground cinnamon
75ml/5 tbsp cocoa powder
200g/7oz/generous 1 cup light muscovado or
demerara sugar
475ml/16fl oz/2 cups milk
crème fraîche, Greek-style yogurt or vanilla
ice cream, to serve

1 Preheat oven to 180°C/350°F/Gas 4. Prepare the dish: use the extra butter to grease a 1.5 litre/2½ pint/6¼ cup ovenproof dish. Place the dish on a baking sheet and set aside.

2 Sift the flour and ground cinnamon into a bowl. Sift in 15ml/1 tbsp of the cocoa and mix well.

3 Place the butter in a saucepan. Add 115g/4oz/½ cup of the sugar and 150ml/¼ pint/⅔ cup of the milk. Heat gently without boiling, stirring from time to time, until the butter has melted and all the sugar has dissolved. Remove the pan from the heat.

4 Stir in the flour mixture, mixing evenly. Pour the mixture into the prepared dish and level the surface.

5 Mix the remaining sugar and cocoa in a bowl, then sprinkle over the pudding mixture.

6 Pour the remaining milk evenly over the pudding.

7 Bake for 45–50 minutes or until the sponge has risen to the top and is firm to the touch. Serve hot, with the crème fraîche, yogurt or ice cream.

Chocolate Crepes with Plums and Port

2 Meanwhile, make the filling. Halve and stone the plums. Place them in a saucepan and add the sugar and water. Bring to the boil, then lower the heat, cover, and simmer for about 10 minutes or until the plums are tender. Stir in the port, taking care not to break up the plums, then simmer for a further 30 seconds. Remove from the heat and keep warm.

3 Have ready a sheet of non-stick baking paper. Heat a crêpe pan, grease it lightly with a little oil, then pour in just enough batter to cover the base of the pan, swirling to coat evenly. Cook until the crêpe has set, then flip it over to cook the other side. Slide the crêpe out on to the sheet of paper, then cook 9–11 more crêpes in the same way. It should not be necessary to add more oil to the pan, but if the crêpes start to stick, add a very light coating.

4 Make the sauce. Combine the chocolate and cream in a saucepan. Heat gently, stirring until smooth. Add the port and heat gently, stirring, for 1 minute.

5 Divide the plum filling among the crêpes, add a dollop of crème fraîche or Greek-style yogurt to each and roll them up carefully. Serve in individual bowls, with the chocolate sauce spooned over the top of each portion.

Serves 6
50g/2oz plain chocolate, chopped into
small pieces
200ml/7fl oz/scant 1 cup milk
120ml/4fl oz/½ cup single cream
30ml/2 tbsp cocoa powder
115g/4oz/1 cup plain flour
2 eggs
oil, for frying

For the Filling
500g/1¼lb red or golden plums
50g/2oz/¼ cup caster sugar
30ml/2 tbsp water
30ml/2 tbsp port
150g/5oz/¾ cup crème fraîche or
Greek-style yogurt

For the Sauce
150g/5oz plain chocolate, chopped into
small pieces
175ml/6fl oz/¾ cup double cream
15ml/1 tbsp port

1 Make the crêpe batter. Place the chocolate in a saucepan with the milk. Heat gently, stirring occasionally, until the chocolate has dissolved. Pour the chocolate and milk mixture into a blender or food processor and add the cream, cocoa, flour and eggs. (If the blender or food processor is a small one, it may be necessary to do this in batches.) Process until smooth, then tip into a jug and chill for 30 minutes.

STEAMED CHOCOLATE AND FRUIT PUDDINGS WITH CHOCOLATE SYRUP

SERVES 4

115g/4oz/⅔ cup dark muscovado sugar
1 eating apple
75g/3oz/¾ cup cranberries, thawed if frozen
115g/4oz/½ cup soft margarine
2 eggs
115g/4oz/½ cup self-raising flour
45ml/3 tbsp cocoa powder

FOR THE CHOCOLATE SYRUP

115g/4oz plain chocolate, chopped
30ml/2 tbsp clear honey
15ml/½oz/1 tbsp unsalted butter
2.5ml/½ tsp vanilla essence

1 Prepare a steamer or half fill a saucepan with water and bring it to the boil. Grease four individual pudding basins and sprinkle each one with a little of the muscovado sugar to coat well all over.

2 Peel and core the apple. Dice it into a bowl, add the cranberries and mix well. Divide the fruit among the prepared pudding basins.

3 Place the remaining muscovado sugar in a mixing bowl. Add the margarine, eggs, flour and cocoa. Beat until combined and smooth.

4 Spoon the mixture into the basins and cover each with a double thickness of foil. Steam for about 45 minutes, topping up the boiling water as required, until the puddings are well risen and firm.

5 Make the syrup. Mix the chocolate, honey, butter and vanilla essence in a small saucepan. Heat gently, stirring until melted and smooth.

6 Run a knife around the edge of each pudding to loosen it, then turn out on to individual plates. Serve at once, with the chocolate syrup.

Chocolate Souffle Crepes

MAKES 12 CREPES

75g / 3oz / ¾ cup plain flour
15ml / 1 tbsp cocoa powder
5ml / 1 tsp caster sugar
pinch of salt
5ml / 1 tsp ground cinnamon
2 eggs
175ml / 6fl oz / ¾ cup milk
5ml / 1 tsp vanilla essence
50g / 2oz / 4 tbsp unsalted butter,
melted
raspberries, pineapple and mint sprigs,
to decorate

FOR THE PINEAPPLE SYRUP

½ medium pineapple, peeled, cored and
finely chopped
120ml / 4fl oz / ½ cup water
30ml / 2 tbsp natural maple syrup
5ml / 1 tsp cornflour
½ cinnamon stick
30ml / 2 tbsp rum

FOR THE SOUFFLE FILLING

250g / 9oz bittersweet chocolate, chopped into
small pieces
75ml / 3fl oz / ⅓ cup double cream
3 eggs, separated
25g / 1oz / 2 tbsp caster sugar

1 Prepare the syrup. In a saucepan over a medium heat, bring the pineapple, water, maple syrup, cornflour and cinnamon stick to the boil. Simmer for 2–3 minutes, until the sauce thickens, whisking frequently. Remove from the heat and discard the cinnamon. Pour into a bowl, and stir in the rum. Cool, then chill.

COOK'S TIP
You might be able to find ready-made crepes in the shops, which will save time.

2 Prepare the crêpes. Sift the flour, cocoa, sugar, salt and cinnamon into a bowl. Stir, then make a well in the centre. In a bowl, beat the eggs, milk and vanilla. Gradually add to the well in the flour mixture, whisking in flour from the side of the bowl to form a smooth batter. Stir in half the melted butter and pour into a jug. Allow to stand for 1 hour.

3 Heat an 18–20 cm / 7–8 in crêpe pan. Brush with butter. Stir the batter. Pour 45ml / 3 tbsp batter into the pan; swirl the pan to cover the bottom. Cook over a medium-high heat for 1–2 minutes until the bottom is golden. Turn over and cook for 30–45 seconds, then turn on to a plate. Stack between sheets of non-stick baking paper and set aside.

4 Prepare the filling. In a saucepan over a medium heat, melt the chocolate and cream until smooth, stirring frequently.

5 In a bowl, with a hand-held electric mixer, beat the yolks with half the sugar for 3–5 minutes, until light and creamy. Gradually beat in the chocolate mixture. Allow to cool. In a separate bowl with cleaned beaters, beat the egg whites until soft peaks form. Gradually beat in the remaining sugar until stiff peaks form. Beat a large spoonful of whites in to the chocolate mixture to lighten it, then fold in the remaining whites.

6 Preheat oven to 200°C / 400°F / Gas 6. Lay a crêpe on a plate, bottom side up. Spoon a little soufflé mixture on to the crêpe, spreading it to the edge. Fold the bottom half over the soufflé mixture, then fold in half again to form a filled triangle. Place on a buttered baking sheet. Repeat with the remaining crêpes. Brush the tops with melted butter and bake for 15–20 minutes, until the filling has souffléd. Decorate with raspberries, pineapple pieces and mint and serve with the syrup.

VARIATION
For a simpler version of the crêpes, just serve with a spoonful of maple syrup rather than making the pineapple syrup.

Chocolate and Orange Scotch Pancakes

Serves 4

115g / 4oz / 1 cup self-raising flour
30ml / 2 tbsp cocoa powder
2 eggs
50g / 2oz plain chocolate, chopped into
small pieces
200ml / 7fl oz / scant 1 cup milk
finely grated rind of 1 orange
30ml / 2 tbsp orange juice
butter or oil, for frying
chocolate curls, to decorate

For the Sauce

2 large oranges
25g / 1oz / 2 tbsp unsalted butter
45ml / 3 tbsp light muscovado sugar
250ml / 8fl oz / 1 cup crème fraîche
30ml / 2 tbsp Grand Marnier or
Cointreau

1 Sift the flour and cocoa into a bowl and make a well in the centre. Add the eggs and beat well, gradually incorporating the surrounding dry ingredients to make a smooth mixture.

2 Mix the chocolate and milk in a saucepan. Heat gently until the chocolate has melted, then beat into the mixture until smooth and bubbly. Stir in the orange rind and juice to make a batter.

3 Heat a large heavy-based frying pan or griddle. Grease with a little butter or oil. Drop large spoonfuls of batter on to the hot surface, leaving room for spreading. Cook over a moderate heat. When the pancakes are lightly browned underneath and bubbly on top, flip over to cook the other side. Slide on to a plate and keep hot, then make more in the same way.

4 Make the sauce. Grate the rind of 1 orange into a bowl and set aside. Peel both oranges, taking care to remove all the pith, then slice the flesh fairly thinly.
5 Heat the butter and sugar in a wide, shallow pan over a low heat, stirring until the sugar dissolves. Stir in the crème fraîche and heat gently.
6 Add the pancakes and orange slices to the sauce, heat gently for 1–2 minutes, then spoon over the liqueur. Sprinkle with the reserved orange rind. Scatter over the chocolate curls and serve the pancakes at once.

Puffy Pears

Serves 4

225g/8oz puff pastry, thawed if frozen
2 pears, peeled
2 squares plain chocolate, roughly chopped
15ml/1 tbsp lemon juice
1 egg, beaten
15ml/1 tbsp caster sugar

1 Roll the pastry into a 25 cm/10 in square on a lightly floured surface. Trim the edges, then cut it into four equal smaller squares. Cover with clear film and set aside.

2 Remove the core from each pear half and pack the gap with the chopped chocolate. Place a pear half, cut-side down, on each piece of pastry and brush them with the lemon juice, to prevent them from going brown.

3 Preheat oven to 190°C/375°F/Gas 5. Cut the pastry into a pear shape, by following the lines of the fruit, leaving a 2.5 cm/1 in border. Use the trimmings to make leaves and brush the pastry border with the beaten egg.

4 Arrange the pastry and pears on a baking sheet. Make deep cuts in the pears, taking care not to cut right through the fruit, and sprinkle them with the sugar. Cook for 20–25 minutes, until lightly browned. Serve hot or cold.

Variation

Use apples instead of pears, if preferred. Cut the pastry into 10 cm/4 in rounds. Slice 2 peeled and cored eating apples. Toss with a little lemon juice, drain and arrange on the pastry. Dot with 25g/1oz/2 tbsp butter and chopped milk chocolate. Bake as for Puffy Pears. While still hot, brush the apple slices with warmed redcurrant jelly.

Pears in Chocolate Fudge Blankets

Serves 6

6 ripe eating pears
30ml/2 tbsp lemon juice
75g/3oz/6 tbsp caster sugar
300ml/½ pint/1¼ cups water
1 cinnamon stick

For the Sauce

200ml/7fl oz/scant 1 cup double cream
150g/5oz/scant 1 cup light muscovado sugar
25g/1oz/2tbsp unsalted butter
25g/1oz/2 tbsp golden syrup
120ml/4fl oz/½ cup milk
200g/7oz plain dark chocolate, broken into squares

1 Peel the pears thinly, leaving the stalks on. Scoop out the cores from the base. Brush the cut surfaces with lemon juice to prevent them from browning.

2 Place the sugar and water in a large saucepan. Heat gently until the sugar dissolves. Add the pears and cinnamon stick with any remaining lemon juice, and, if necessary, a little more water, so that the pears are almost covered.

3 Bring to the boil, then lower the heat, cover the pan and simmer the pears gently for 15–20 minutes or until they are just tender when pierced with a slim skewer.

4 Meanwhile, make the sauce. Place the cream, sugar, butter, golden syrup and milk in a heavy-based saucepan. Heat gently until the sugar has dissolved and the butter and syrup have melted, then bring to the boil. Boil, stirring constantly, for about 5 minutes or until the sauce is thick. Remove from the heat and stir in the chocolate, a few squares at a time, until melted.

5 Using a slotted spoon, transfer the poached pears to a dish. Keep hot. Boil the syrup rapidly to reduce to about 45–60ml/3–4 tbsp. Remove the cinnamon stick and stir the syrup into the chocolate sauce. Serve poured over the pears in individual bowls.

RICH CHOCOLATE BERRY TART WITH BLACKBERRY SAUCE

SERVES 10

115g/4oz/½ cup unsalted butter, softened

115g/4oz/½ cup caster sugar

2.5ml/½ tsp salt

15ml/1 tbsp vanilla essence

50g/2oz/½ cup cocoa powder

175g/6oz/1½ cups plain flour

450g/1 lb fresh berries, for topping

FOR THE CHOCOLATE GANACHE FILLING

475ml/16fl oz/2 cups double cream

150g/5oz/½ cup blackberry or raspberry jelly

225g/8oz bittersweet chocolate, chopped into small pieces

25g/1oz/2 tbsp unsalted butter, cut into small pieces

FOR THE BLACKBERRY SAUCE

225g/8oz fresh or frozen blackberries or raspberries

15ml/1 tbsp lemon juice

30ml/2 tbsp caster sugar

30ml/2 tbsp blackberry- or raspberry-flavoured liqueur

1 In a food processor fitted with a metal blade, process the butter, sugar, salt and vanilla essence until creamy. Add the cocoa and process for 1 minute. Add the flour all at once, then pulse for 10–15 seconds. Place a piece of clear film on the work surface. Turn the dough out on to this, shape into a flat disc and wrap tightly. Chill for 1 hour.

2 Lightly grease a 23 cm/9 in flan tin with a removable base. Let the dough soften for 5–10 minutes, then roll out between two sheets of clear film to a 28 cm/11 in round, about 5 mm/¼ in thick. Peel off the top sheet of clear film and invert the dough into the prepared tin. Ease the dough into the tin, and when in position lift off the clear film.

3 With floured fingers, press the dough on to the base and sides of the tin, then roll the rolling pin over the edge to cut off any excess dough. Prick the base of the dough with a fork. Chill for 1 hour. Preheat oven to 180°C/350°F/Gas 4. Line the pastry case with non-stick baking paper; fill with baking beans and bake blind for 10 minutes. Remove the paper and beans and bake for 5 minutes more, until the pastry is just set. Cool in the tin on a wire rack.

4 Prepare the ganache filling. In a medium saucepan over a medium heat, bring the cream and berry jelly to the boil. Remove from the heat and add the chocolate all at once, stirring until melted and smooth. Stir in the butter until melted, then strain into the cooled tart shell, smoothing the top. Cool the tart completely.

5 Prepare the sauce. Process the berries, lemon juice and sugar in a food processor until smooth. Strain into a small bowl and add the liqueur.

6 To serve, remove the tart from the tin. Place on a serving plate and arrange the berries on top of the tart. With a pastry brush, brush the berries with a little of the blackberry sauce to glaze lightly. Serve the remaining sauce separately.

CHOCOLATE TRUFFLE TART

SERVES 12

115g/4oz/1 cup plain flour
30g/1¼oz/⅓ cup cocoa powder
50g/2oz/¼ cup caster sugar
2.5ml/½ tsp salt
115g/4oz/½ cup unsalted butter, cut
into pieces
1 egg yolk
15–30ml/1–2 tbsp iced water
25g/1oz fine quality white or milk chocolate,
melted
whipped cream for serving (optional)
FOR THE TRUFFLE FILLING
350ml/12fl oz/1½ cups double cream
350g/12oz couverture or fine quality
bittersweet chocolate, chopped
50g/2oz/4 tbsp unsalted butter, cut into
small pieces
30ml/2 tbsp brandy or liqueur

1 Prepare the pastry. Sift the flour and cocoa into a bowl. In a food processor fitted with a metal blade, process the flour mixture with the sugar and salt. Add the butter and process for 15–20 seconds, until the mixture resembles coarse breadcrumbs.

2 In a bowl, lightly beat the yolk with the iced water. Add to the flour mixture and pulse until the dough begins to stick together. Turn out the dough on to a sheet of clear film. Use the film to help shape the dough into a flat disc. Wrap tightly. Chill for 1–2 hours, until firm.

3 Lightly grease a 23 cm/9 in tart tin with a removable base. Let the dough soften briefly, then roll it out between sheets of waxed paper or clear film to a 28 cm/11 in round, about 5 mm/¼ in thick. Peel off the top sheet and invert the dough into a tart tin. Remove the bottom sheet. Ease the dough into the tin. Prick with a fork. Chill for 1 hour.

4 Preheat oven to 180°C/350°F/Gas 4. Line the tart with foil or non-stick baking paper; fill with baking beans. Bake blind for 5–7 minutes. Lift out the foil with the beans, return the pastry case to the oven and bake for a further 5–7 minutes, until the pastry is just set. Cool completely in the tin on a rack.

5 Prepare the filling. In a medium pan over a medium heat, bring the cream to the boil. Remove the pan from the heat and stir in the chocolate until melted and smooth. Stir in the butter and brandy or liqueur. Strain into the prepared tart shell, tilting the tin slightly to level the surface. Do not touch the surface of the filling or it will spoil the glossy finish.

6 Spoon the melted chocolate into a paper piping bag and cut off the tip. Drop rounds of chocolate over the surface of the tart and use a skewer or toothpick to draw a point gently through the chocolate to produce a marbled effect. Chill for 2–3 hours, until set. To serve, allow the tart to soften slightly at room temperature.

MARBLED CHOCOLATE CHEESECAKE

SERVES 6

50g / 2oz / ½ cup cocoa powder
75ml / 5 tbsp hot water
900g / 2lb cream cheese, at room temperature
200g / 7oz / scant 1 cup caster sugar
4 eggs
5ml / 1 tsp vanilla essence
75g / 3oz digestive biscuits, crushed

1 Preheat oven to 180°C/350°F/Gas 4. Line a 20 x 8 cm/8 x 3 in cake tin with greaseproof paper. Grease the paper.
2 Sift the cocoa powder into a bowl. Pour over the hot water and stir to dissolve.
3 Beat the cheese until smooth, then beat in the sugar, followed by the eggs, one at a time. Do not overmix.
4 Divide the mixture evenly between two bowls. Stir the chocolate mixture into one bowl, then add the vanilla essence to the remaining mixture.

5 Pour a cup or ladleful of the plain mixture into the centre of the tin; it will spread out into an even layer. Slowly pour over a cupful of chocolate mixture in the centre. Continue to alternate the cake mixtures in this way until both are used up. Draw a thin metal skewer through the cake mixture for a marbled effect.
6 Set the tin in a roasting pan and pour in hot water to come 4 cm/1½ in up the sides of the cake tin.

7 Bake the cheesecake for about 1½ hours, until the top is golden. (The cake will rise during baking but will sink later.) Cool in the tin on a wire rack.
8 Run a knife around the inside edge of the cake. Invert a flat plate over the tin and turn out the cake.

9 Sprinkle the crushed biscuits evenly over the cake, gently invert another plate on top, and turn over again. Cover and chill for 3 hours, preferably overnight.

BLACK BOTTOM PIE

SERVES 6–8

250g / 9oz / 2¼ cups plain flour
150g / 5oz / ⅔ cup unsalted butter
2 egg yolks
15–30ml / 1–2 tbsp iced water
FOR THE FILLING
3 eggs, separated
20ml / 4 tsp cornflour
75g / 3oz / 6 tbsp golden caster sugar
400ml / 14fl oz / 1⅔ cups milk
*150g / 5oz plain chocolate, chopped into
small pieces*
5ml / 1 tsp vanilla essence
1 sachet powdered gelatine
45ml / 3 tbsp water
30ml / 2 tbsp dark rum
FOR THE TOPPING
*175ml / 6 fl oz / ¾ cup double cream or
whipping cream*
chocolate curls

1 Sift the flour into a bowl and rub in the butter until the mixture resembles coarse breadcrumbs. Stir in the egg yolks with just enough iced water to bind the mixture to a soft dough. Roll out on a lightly floured surface and line a deep 23 cm / 9 in flan tin. Chill the pastry case for about 30 minutes.
2 Preheat oven to 190°C/375°F/Gas 5. Prick the pastry case all over with a fork, cover with greaseproof paper weighed down with baking beans and bake blind for 10 minutes. Remove the baking beans and paper, return the pastry case to the oven and bake for a further 10 minutes, until the pastry is crisp and golden. Cool in the tin.

POTS AU CHOCOLAT
The chocolate and chestnut mixture (minus the pastry) also makes delicious individual *pots au chocolat*. Make the fillings as described above; then simply pour the mixture into small ramekins that have been lightly greased with butter. Decorate with a blob of whipped cream and grated chocolate and serve with *langues de chat*.

CHOCOLATE AND CHESTNUT PIE
*23 cm / 9 in pastry case (see recipe
above), cooked*
FOR THE FILLING
115g / 4oz / ½ cup butter, softened
115g / 4oz / ¼ cup caster sugar
*425g / 15oz can unsweetened chestnut
purée*
*225g / 8oz plain chocolate, broken into
small pieces*
30ml / 2 tbsp brandy

1 Make the filling. Cream the butter with the caster sugar in a mixing bowl until pale and fluffy. Add the unsweetened chestnut purée, about 30ml / 2 tbsp at a time, beating well after each addition.
2 Put the chocolate in a heatproof bowl. Place over a saucepan of barely simmering water until the chocolate has melted, stirring occasionally until smooth. Stir the chocolate into the chestnut mixture until combined, then add the brandy.
3 Pour the filling into the cold pastry case. Using a spatula, level the surface. Chill until set. Decorate with whipped cream and chocolate leaves, if desired, or simply add a dusting of sifted cocoa.

3 Make the filling. Mix the egg yolks, cornflour and 30ml / 2 tbsp of the sugar in a bowl. Heat the milk in a saucepan until almost boiling, then beat into the egg mixture. Return to the clean pan and stir over a low heat until the custard has thickened and is smooth. Pour half the custard into a bowl.

4 Put the chocolate in a heatproof bowl. Place over a saucepan of barely simmering water until the chocolate has melted, stirring occasionally until smooth. Stir the melted chocolate into the custard in the bowl, with the vanilla essence. Spread the filling in the pastry case and cover closely with dampened greaseproof paper or clear film to prevent the formation of a skin. Allow to cool, then chill until set.

5 Sprinkle the gelatine over the water in a bowl, leave until spongy, then place the bowl over a pan of simmering water until all the gelatine has dissolved. Stir into the remaining custard, then add the rum. Whisk the egg whites in a clean, grease-free bowl until peaks form. Whisk in the remaining sugar, a little at a time, until stiff, then fold the egg whites quickly but evenly into the rum-flavoured custard.
6 Spoon the rum-flavoured custard over the chocolate layer in the pastry case. Using a spatula, level the mixture, making sure that none of the chocolate custard is visible. Return the pie to the fridge until the top layer has set, then remove the pie from the tin and place it on a serving plate. Whip the cream, spread it over the pie and sprinkle with chocolate curls, to decorate.

LUXURY WHITE CHOCOLATE CHEESECAKE

SERVES 16–20

150g / 5oz (about 16–18) digestive biscuits
50g / 2oz / ½ cup blanched hazelnuts, toasted
50g / 2oz / ¼ cup unsalted butter, melted
2.5ml / ½ tsp ground cinnamon
white chocolate curls, to decorate
cocoa powder, for dusting (optional)

FOR THE FILLING

350g / 12oz fine quality white chocolate,
chopped into small pieces
120ml / 4fl oz / ½ cup whipping cream or
double cream
675g / 1½lb / 3 x 8oz packets cream
cheese, softened
50g / 2oz / ¼ cup granulated sugar
4 eggs
30ml / 2 tbsp hazelnut-flavoured liqueur or
15ml / 1 tbsp vanilla essence

FOR THE TOPPING

450ml / ¾ pint / 1¾ cups soured cream
50g / 2oz / ¼ cup granulated sugar
15ml / 1 tbsp hazelnut-flavoured liqueur or
5ml / 1 tsp vanilla essence

3 Using a hand-held electric mixer, beat the cream cheese and sugar in a large bowl until smooth. Add the eggs one at a time, beating well. Slowly beat in the white chocolate mixture and liqueur or vanilla essence. Pour the filling into the baked crust. Place the tin on the hot baking sheet. Bake for 45–55 minutes, and do not allow the top to brown. Transfer the cheesecake to a wire rack while preparing the topping. Increase the oven temperature to 200°C/400°F/Gas 6.

4 Prepare the topping. In a small bowl whisk the soured cream, sugar and liqueur or vanilla essence until thoroughly mixed. Pour the mixture over the cheesecake, spreading it evenly, and return to the oven. Bake for a further 5–7 minutes. Turn off the oven, but do not open the door for 1 hour. Serve the cheesecake at room temperature, decorated with the white chocolate curls. Dust the surface lightly with cocoa powder, if desired.

1 Preheat oven to 180°C/350°F/Gas 4. Grease a 23 x 7.5 cm/9 x 3 in springform tin. In a food processor, process the biscuits and hazelnuts until fine crumbs form. Pour in the butter and cinnamon. Process just until blended. Using the back of a spoon, press on to the base and to within 1 cm/½ in of the top of the sides of the cake tin. Bake the crumb crust for 5–7 minutes, until just set. Cool in the tin on a wire rack. Lower the oven temperature to 150°C/300°F/Gas 2 and place a baking sheet inside to heat up.

2 Prepare the filling. In a small saucepan over a low heat, melt the white chocolate and cream until smooth, stirring frequently. Set aside to cool slightly.

CHOCOLATE TIRAMISU TART

SERVES 12–16

115g/4oz/½ cup unsalted butter
15ml/1 tbsp coffee-flavoured liqueur or water
175g/6oz/1½ cups plain flour
25g/1oz/¼ cup cocoa powder
25g/1oz/¼ cup icing sugar
pinch of salt
2.5ml/½ tsp vanilla essence
cocoa powder, for dusting

FOR THE CHOCOLATE LAYER

350ml/12fl oz/1½ cups double cream
15ml/1 tbsp golden syrup
115g/4oz bittersweet chocolate, chopped into small pieces
25g/1oz/2 tbsp unsalted butter, cut into small pieces
30ml/2 tbsp coffee-flavoured liqueur

FOR THE FILLING

250ml/8fl oz/1 cup whipping cream
350g/12oz/1½ cups mascarpone cheese, at room temperature
45ml/3 tbsp icing sugar
45ml/3 tbsp cold espresso or strong black coffee
45ml/3 tbsp coffee-flavoured liqueur
90g/3½oz plain chocolate, grated

1 Make the pastry. Lightly grease a 23 cm/9 in springform tin. In a saucepan, heat the butter and liqueur or water until the butter has melted. Sift the flour, cocoa, icing sugar and salt into a bowl. Remove the butter mixture from the heat, stir in the vanilla essence and gradually stir into the flour mixture until a soft dough forms.

2 Knead lightly until smooth. Press on to the base and up the sides of the tin to within 2 cm/¾ in of the top. Prick the dough. Chill for 40 minutes. Preheat oven to 190°C/375°F/Gas 5. Bake the pastry case for 8–10 minutes. If the pastry puffs up, prick it with a fork and bake for 2–3 minutes more until set. Cool in the tin on a rack.

3 Prepare the chocolate layer. Bring the cream and syrup to a boil in a pan over a medium heat. Off the heat, add the chocolate, stirring until melted. Beat in the butter and liqueur and pour into the pastry case. Cool completely, then chill.

4 Prepare the filling. Using a hand-held electric mixer, whip the cream in a bowl until soft peaks form. In another bowl, beat the cheese until soft, then beat in the icing sugar until smooth and creamy. Gradually beat in the cold coffee and liqueur; gently fold in the whipped cream and chocolate. Spoon the filling into the pastry case, on top of the chocolate layer. Level the surface. Chill until ready to serve.

5 To serve, run a sharp knife around the side of the tin to loosen the tart shell. Remove the side of the tin and slide the tart on to a plate. Sift a layer of cocoa powder over the tart to decorate, or pipe rosettes of whipped cream around the rim and top each with a chocolate-coated coffee bean. Chocolate Tiramisu Tart is very rich, so serve it in small wedges, with cups of espresso.

RASPBERRY, MASCARPONE AND WHITE CHOCOLATE CHEESECAKE

SERVES 8
50g / 2oz / ¼ cup unsalted butter
225g / 8oz ginger biscuits, crushed
*50g / 2oz / ½ cup chopped pecan nuts
or walnuts*
FOR THE FILLING
275g / 10oz / 1¼ cups mascarpone cheese
175g / 6oz / ¾ cup fromage frais
2 eggs, beaten
45ml / 3 tbsp caster sugar
*250g / 9oz white chocolate, chopped into
small pieces*
225g / 8oz / 1½ cups fresh or frozen raspberries
FOR THE TOPPING
115g / 4oz / ½ cup mascarpone cheese
75g / 3oz / ⅓ cup fromage frais
*white chocolate curls and fresh raspberries,
to decorate*

<u>1</u> Preheat oven to 150°C/300°F/Gas 2. Melt the butter in a saucepan, then stir in the crushed biscuits and nuts. Press into the base of a 23 cm/9 in springform cake tin. Level the surface.

<u>2</u> Make the filling. Using a wooden spoon, beat the mascarpone and fromage frais in a large mixing bowl, then beat in the eggs, a little at a time. Add the caster sugar. Beat until the sugar has dissolved, and the mixture is smooth and creamy.

<u>3</u> Melt the white chocolate gently in a heatproof bowl over a saucepan of simmering water, then stir into the cheese mixture. Add the fresh or frozen raspberries and mix lightly.

<u>4</u> Tip into the prepared tin and spread evenly, then bake for about 1 hour or until just set. Switch off the oven, but do not remove the cheesecake. Leave it until cold and completely set.

<u>5</u> Remove the sides of the tin and carefully lift the cheesecake on to a serving plate. Make the topping by mixing the mascarpone and fromage frais in a bowl and spreading the mixture over the cheesecake. Decorate with chocolate curls and raspberries.

APRICOT AND WHITE CHOCOLATE CHEESECAKE

Use 225g/8oz/1 cup ready-to-eat dried apricots instead of the fresh or frozen raspberries in the cheesecake mixture. Slice the apricots thinly or dice them. Omit the mascarpone and fromage frais topping and serve the cheesecake with an apricot sauce, made by poaching 225g/8oz stoned fresh apricots in 120ml/4fl oz/½ cup water until tender, then rubbing the fruit and liquid through a sieve placed over a bowl. Sweeten the apricot purée with caster sugar to taste, and add enough lemon juice to sharpen the flavour. Alternatively, purée drained canned apricots with a little of their syrup, then stir in lemon juice to taste.

MISSISSIPPI MUD PIE

SERVES 8

175g / 6oz / 1½ cups plain flour
2.5ml / ½ tsp salt
115g / 4oz / ½ cup butter
30–45ml / 2–3 tbsp iced water

FOR THE FILLING

75g / 3oz plain chocolate, broken into small pieces
50g / 2oz / ¼ cup butter or margarine
45ml / 3 tbsp golden syrup
3 eggs, beaten
150g / 5oz / ⅔ cup soft light brown sugar
5ml / 1 tsp vanilla essence

TO DECORATE

115g / 4oz chocolate bar
300ml / ½ pint / 1¼ cups whipping cream

<u>1</u> Preheat oven to 220°C/425°F/Gas 7. Sift the flour and salt into a mixing bowl. Rub in the butter until the mixture resembles coarse breadcrumbs. Sprinkle in the water, about 15ml/1 tbsp at a time, and toss the mixture lightly with your fingers or a fork until the dough forms a ball.

<u>2</u> On a lightly floured surface, roll out the pastry and line a 23 cm/9 in flan tin, easing in the pastry and being careful not to stretch it. With your thumbs, make a fluted edge.

<u>3</u> Using a fork, prick the base and sides of the pastry case. Bake for 10–15 minutes, until lightly browned. Cool, in the pan.

<u>4</u> Make the filling. In a heatproof bowl set over a pan of barely simmering water, melt the plain chocolate with the butter or margarine and the golden syrup. Remove the bowl from the heat and stir in the eggs, sugar and vanilla essence.

<u>5</u> Lower the oven temperature to 180°C/350°F/Gas 4. Pour the chocolate mixture into the pastry case. Bake for 35–40 minutes, until the filling is set. Allow to cool completely in the flan tin, on a rack.

<u>6</u> Make the decoration. Use the heat of your hands to soften the chocolate bar slightly. Working over a sheet of non-stick baking paper, draw the blade of a swivel-bladed vegetable peeler across the side of the chocolate bar to shave off short, wide curls. Chill the curls until required.

<u>7</u> Before serving the pie, pour the cream into a bowl and whip to soft peaks. Spread over the top of the pie, hiding the chocolate filling completely. Decorate with the chocolate curls.

ITALIAN CHOCOLATE RICOTTA PIE

SERVES 6

225g / 8oz / 2 cups plain flour
30ml / 2 tbsp cocoa powder
60ml / 4 tbsp caster sugar
115g / 4oz / ½ cup unsalted butter
60ml / 4 tbsp dry sherry

FOR THE FILLING

2 egg yolks
115g / 4oz / ½ cup caster sugar
500g / 1¼lb / 2½ cups ricotta cheese
finely grated rind of 1 lemon
90ml / 6 tbsp dark chocolate chips
75ml / 5 tbsp chopped mixed peel
45ml / 3 tbsp chopped angelica

1 Sift the flour and cocoa into a bowl, then stir in the sugar. Rub in the butter using your fingertips, then work in the sherry to make a firm dough.

2 Preheat oven to 200°C / 400°F / Gas 6. Roll out three-quarters of the pastry on a lightly floured surface and line a 24 cm / 9½ in loose-based flan tin.

3 Make the filling. Beat the egg yolks and sugar in a bowl, then beat in the ricotta to mix thoroughly. Stir in the lemon rind, chocolate chips, mixed peel and angelica.

4 Scrape the ricotta mixture into the pastry case and level the surface. Roll out the remaining pastry and cut into strips. Arrange these in a lattice over the pie.

5 Bake for 15 minutes. Lower the oven temperature to 180°C / 350°F / Gas 4 and cook for a further 30–35 minutes, until golden brown and firm. Cool the pie in the tin. Serve at room temperature.

WHITE CHOCOLATE AND MANGO CREAM TART

SERVES 8

175g / 6oz / 1½ cups plain flour
75g / 3oz / 1 cup sweetened, desiccated coconut
115g / 4oz / ½ cup butter, softened
30ml / 2 tbsp caster sugar
2 egg yolks
2.5ml / ½ tsp almond essence
600ml / 1 pint / 2½ cups whipping cream
1 large ripe mango
50g / 2oz / ½ cup toasted flaked almonds,
to decorate

FOR THE WHITE CHOCOLATE CUSTARD FILLING

150g / 5oz fine quality white chocolate,
chopped into small pieces
120ml / 4fl oz / ½ cup whipping cream or
double cream
75ml / 5 tbsp cornflour
15ml / 1 tbsp plain flour
50g / 2oz / ¼ cup granulated sugar
350ml / 12fl oz / 1½ cups milk
5 egg yolks

1 Using a hand-held electric mixer at low speed, beat the flour, coconut, butter, sugar, egg yolks and almond essence in a deep bowl until the mixture forms a soft dough. Lightly grease a 23 cm / 9 in tart tin with a removable base. Press the pastry on to the bottom and sides. Prick the pastry case with a fork. Chill the case for 30 minutes.

COOK'S TIP

Choose a mango that is a rich yellow in colour, with a pink or red blush. It should just yield to the touch, but should not be too soft. Peel it carefully, then cut it in half around the stone. Cut each piece in half again, then in neat slices.

2 Preheat oven to 180°C / 350°F / Gas 4. Line the pastry case with non-stick baking paper; fill with baking beans and bake blind for 10 minutes. Remove the paper and beans and bake for a further 5–7 minutes, until golden. Cool the cooked pastry in the tin on a wire rack.

3 Prepare the custard filling. In a small saucepan over a low heat, melt the white chocolate with the cream, stirring until smooth. Set aside. Combine the cornflour, plain flour and sugar in a medium saucepan. Stir in the milk gradually. Place over a medium heat and cook, stirring constantly, until the mixture has thickened.

4 Beat the egg yolks in a small bowl. Slowly add about 250ml / 8fl oz / 1 cup of the hot milk mixture, stirring constantly. Return the yolk mixture to the rest of the sauce in the pan, stirring constantly.

5 Bring the custard filling to a gentle boil, stirring constantly until thickened. Stir in the melted white chocolate until well blended. Cool to room temperature, stirring frequently to prevent a skin from forming on the surface. Beat the whipping cream in a medium-sized bowl until soft peaks form. Fold approximately 120ml / 4fl oz / ½ cup of the whipped cream into the white chocolate custard and spoon half the custard into the base. Peel and slice the mango thinly.

6 With the aid of a slim metal spatula or palette knife, arrange the mango slices over the custard in concentric circles, starting at the rim and then filling in the centre. Try to avoid moving the mango slices once in position. Carefully pour the remaining custard over the mango slices, smoothing the surface evenly. Remove the side of the tin and slide the tart carefully on to a serving plate.

7 Spoon the remaining flavoured cream into a large piping bag fitted with a medium star tip. Pipe the cream in a scroll pattern in parallel rows on top of the tart, keeping the rows about 1 cm / ½ in apart. Carefully sprinkle the toasted flaked almonds between the rows. Serve the tart chilled.

Hazelnut Chocolate Meringue Torte with Pears

Serves 8–10

175g/6oz/¾ cup granulated sugar
1 vanilla pod, split
475ml/6fl oz/2 cups water
4 ripe pears, peeled, halved and cored
30ml/2 tbsp hazelnut- or pear-flavoured liqueur
150g/5oz/1¼ cups hazelnuts, toasted
6 egg whites
pinch of salt
350g/12oz/2¼ cups icing sugar
5ml/1 tsp vanilla essence
50g/2oz plain chocolate, melted

For the Chocolate Cream

275g/10oz fine quality bittersweet or plain chocolate, chopped into small pieces
475ml/16fl oz/2 cups whipping cream
60ml/4 tbsp hazelnut- or pear-flavoured liqueur

1 In a saucepan large enough to hold the pears in a single layer combine the sugar, vanilla pod and water. Over a high heat, bring to the boil, stirring until the sugar dissolves. Lower the heat, add the pears to the syrup, cover and simmer gently for 12–15 minutes until tender. Remove the pan from the heat and allow the pears to cool in their poaching liquid. Carefully lift the pears out of the liquid and drain on kitchen paper. Transfer them to a plate, sprinkle with liqueur, cover and chill overnight.

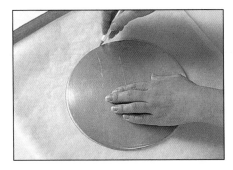

2 Preheat oven to 180°C/350°F/Gas 4. With a pencil draw a 23 cm/9 in circle on each of two sheets of non-stick baking paper. Turn the paper over on to two baking sheets (so that the pencil marks are underneath). Crumb the toasted hazelnuts in a food processor fitted with a metal blade.

3 In a large bowl, beat the whites with a hand-held electric mixer until frothy. Add the salt and beat on high speed until soft peaks form. Reduce the mixer speed and gradually add the icing sugar, beating well after each addition until all the sugar has been added and the whites are stiff and glossy; this will take 12–15 minutes. Gently fold in the nuts and vanilla essence and spoon the meringue on to the circles on the baking sheets, smoothing the top and sides.

4 Bake for 1 hour until the tops are dry and firm. Turn off the oven and allow to cool in the oven for 2–3 hours or overnight, until completely dry.

5 Prepare the chocolate cream. Melt the chocolate in a heatproof bowl set over a saucepan of simmering water. Stir the chocolate until melted and smooth. Cool to room temperature. Using a hand-held electric mixer beat the cream in a bowl to form soft peaks. Quickly fold the cream into the melted chocolate; fold in the liqueur. Spoon about one third of the chocolate cream into an icing bag fitted with a star tip. Set aside.

6 Thinly slice each pear half lengthwise with a sharp knife. Place one meringue layer on a serving plate. Spread with half the chocolate cream and arrange half the sliced pears evenly over the cream. Pipe a border of rosettes around the edge.

7 Top with the second meringue layer and spread with the remaining chocolate cream. Arrange the remaining pear slices in an attractive pattern over the chocolate cream. Pipe a border of rosettes around the edge. Spoon the melted chocolate into a small paper cone and drizzle the chocolate over the pears. Chill for at least 1 hour before serving.

CHOCOLATE, BANANA AND TOFFEE PIE

SERVES 6
65g / 2½oz / 5 tbsp unsalted butter,
melted
250g / 9oz milk chocolate digestive biscuits,
crushed
chocolate curls, to decorate
FOR THE FILLING
397g / 13oz can condensed milk
150g / 5oz plain chocolate, chopped
120ml / 4fl oz / ½ cup crème fraîche
15ml / 1 tbsp golden syrup
FOR THE TOPPING
2 bananas
250ml / 8fl oz / 1 cup crème fraîche
10ml / 2 tsp strong black coffee

1 Mix the butter with the biscuit crumbs. Press on to the base and sides of a 23cm / 9in loose-based flan tin. Chill.

2 Make the filling. Place the unopened can of condensed milk in a deep saucepan of boiling water, making sure that it is completely covered. Lower the heat and simmer, covered for 2 hours, topping up the water as necessary. The can must remain covered at all times.

3 Remove the pan from the heat and set aside, covered, until the can has cooled down completely in the water. Do not attempt to open the can until it is completely cold.

4 Gently melt the chocolate with the crème fraîche and golden syrup in a heatproof bowl over a saucepan of simmering water. Stir in the caramelized condensed milk and beat until evenly mixed. Pour the filling into the biscuit crust and spread it evenly.

5 Slice the bananas evenly and arrange them over the chocolate filling.

6 Stir the crème fraîche and coffee together in a bowl, then spoon the mixture over the bananas. Sprinkle the chocolate curls on top. Alternatively, omit the crème fraîche topping and decorate with whipped cream and extra banana slices.

COLD DESSERTS

CHOCOLATE PROFITEROLES

4 Beat 1 egg in a small bowl and set aside. Add the whole eggs, one at a time, to the flour mixture, beating well after each addition. Beat in just enough of the beaten egg to make a smooth, shiny dough. It should pull away and fall slowly when dropped from a spoon.

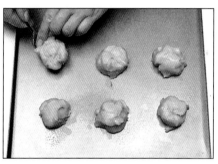

5 Using a tablespoon, ease the dough in 12 mounds on to the prepared baking sheet. Bake for 25–30 minutes, until the puffs are golden brown.

6 Remove the puffs from the oven and cut a small slit in the side of each of them to release the steam. Return the puffs to the oven, turn off the heat and leave them to dry out, with the oven door open.

7 Remove the ice cream from the freezer and allow it to soften for about 10 minutes. Split the profiteroles in half and put a small scoop of ice cream in each. Arrange on a serving platter or divide among individual plates. Pour the sauce over the profiteroles and serve at once.

SERVES 4-6

110g / 3¾oz / scant 1 cup plain flour
1.5ml / ¼ tsp salt
pinch of freshly grated nutmeg
175ml / 6fl oz / ¾ cup water
75g / 3oz / 6 tbsp unsalted butter, cut into 6 equal pieces
3 eggs
750ml / 1¼ pints / 3 cups vanilla ice cream

FOR THE CHOCOLATE SAUCE

275g / 10oz plain chocolate, chopped into small pieces
120ml / 4fl oz / ½ cup warm water

1 Preheat oven to 200°C/400°F/Gas 6. Grease a baking sheet. Sift the flour, salt and nutmeg on to a sheet of greaseproof paper or foil.

2 Make the sauce. Melt the chocolate with the water in a heatproof bowl placed over a saucepan of barely simmering water. Stir until smooth. Keep warm until ready to serve, or reheat when required.

3 In a medium saucepan, bring the water and butter to the boil. Remove from the heat and add the dry ingredients all at once, funnelling them in from the paper or foil. Beat with a wooden spoon for about 1 minute until well blended and the mixture starts to pull away from the pan, then set the pan over a low heat and cook the mixture for about 2 minutes, beating constantly. Remove from the heat.

VARIATION
Fill the profiteroles with whipped cream, if you prefer. Spoon the cream into a piping bag and fill the slit puffs, or sandwich the halved puffs with the cream.

CHOCOLATE CONES WITH APRICOT SAUCE

SERVES 6

*250g / 9oz plain dark chocolate, chopped into
small pieces*
350g / 12oz / 1½ cups ricotta cheese
45ml / 3 tbsp double cream
30ml / 2 tbsp brandy
30ml / 2 tbsp icing sugar
finely grated rind of 1 lemon
pared strips of lemon rind, to decorate
FOR THE SAUCE
175g / 6oz / ⅔ cup apricot jam
45ml / 3 tbsp lemon juice

<u>1</u> Cut twelve 10 cm / 4 in double
thickness rounds from non-stick baking
paper and shape each into a cone. Secure
with masking tape.
<u>2</u> Melt the chocolate over a saucepan of
simmering water. Cool slightly, then
spoon a little into each cone, swirling and
brushing it to coat the paper evenly.

<u>3</u> Support each cone point downwards in
a cup or glass held on its side, to keep it
level. Leave in a cool place until the cones
are completely set. Unless it is a very hot
day, do not put the cones in the fridge, as
this may mar their appearance.
<u>4</u> Make the sauce. Combine the apricot
jam and lemon juice in a small saucepan.
Melt over a gentle heat, stirring
occasionally, then press through a sieve
into a small bowl. Set aside to cool.

<u>5</u> Beat the ricotta cheese in a bowl until
softened, then beat in the cream, brandy
and icing sugar. Stir in the lemon rind.
Spoon the mixture into a piping bag. Fill
the cones, then carefully peel off the non-
stick baking paper.
<u>6</u> Spoon a pool of apricot sauce on to six
dessert plates. Arrange the cones in pairs
on the plates. Decorate with a scattering
of pared lemon rind strips and serve
immediately.

CHOCOLATE HAZELNUT GALETTES

SERVES 4

175g/6oz plain chocolate, chopped into small pieces

45ml/3 tbsp single cream

30ml/2 tbsp flaked hazelnuts

115g/4oz white chocolate, chopped into small pieces

175g/6oz/¾ cup fromage frais (8% fat)

15ml/1 tbsp dry sherry

60ml/4 tbsp finely chopped hazelnuts, toasted physalis (Cape gooseberries), dipped in white chocolate, to decorate

1 Melt the plain chocolate in a heatproof bowl over a saucepan of barely simmering water, then remove the pan from the heat and lift off the bowl. Stir the cream into the melted chocolate. Draw twelve 7.5 cm/3 in circles on sheets of non-stick baking paper.

2 Turn the baking paper over and spread the plain chocolate over each marked circle, covering in a thin, even layer. Scatter flaked hazelnuts over four of the circles, then leave until set.

3 Melt the white chocolate in a heatproof bowl over hot water, then stir in the fromage frais and dry sherry. Fold in the chopped, toasted hazelnuts. Leave to cool until the mixture holds its shape.

4 Remove the plain chocolate rounds carefully from the paper and sandwich them together in stacks of three, spooning the white chocolate hazelnut cream between the layers and using the hazelnut-covered rounds on top. Chill before serving.

5 To serve, place the galettes on individual plates and decorate with chocolate-dipped physalis.

CHOCOLATE VANILLA TIMBALES

SERVES 6

350ml/12fl oz/1½ cups semi-skimmed milk
30ml/2 tbsp cocoa powder
2 eggs
10ml/2 tsp vanilla essence
45ml/3 tbsp granulated sweetener
15ml/1 tbsp/1 sachet powdered gelatine
45ml/3 tbsp hot water
extra cocoa powder, to decorate

FOR THE SAUCE

115g/4oz/½ cup light Greek-style yogurt
25ml/1½ tbsp vanilla essence

<u>1</u> Place the milk and cocoa powder in a saucepan and stir until the milk is boiling. Separate the eggs and beat the egg yolks with the vanilla and sweetener in a bowl, until the mixture is pale and smooth. Gradually pour in the chocolate milk, beating well.

<u>2</u> Return the mixture to the pan and stir constantly over a gentle heat, without boiling, until it is slightly thickened and smooth.

<u>3</u> Remove the pan from the heat. Pour the gelatine into the hot water and stir until it is completely dissolved, then quickly stir it into the milk mixture. Put this mixture aside and allow it to cool until almost setting.

<u>4</u> Whisk the egg whites until they hold soft peaks. Fold the egg whites quickly into the milk mixture. Spoon the timbale mixture into six individual moulds and chill them until set.

<u>5</u> To serve, run a knife around the edge, dip the moulds quickly into hot water and turn out. Dust with cocoa. For the sauce, stir together the yogurt and vanilla and spoon on to the plates.

TIRAMISU IN CHOCOLATE CUPS

SERVES 6

1 egg yolk
30ml / 2 tbsp caster sugar
2.5ml / ½ tsp vanilla essence
250g / 9oz / generous 1 cup mascarpone cheese
120ml / 4fl oz / ½ cup strong black coffee
15ml / 1 tbsp cocoa powder
30ml / 2 tbsp coffee liqueur
16 amaretti biscuits
cocoa powder, for dusting

FOR THE CHOCOLATE CUPS
175g / 6oz plain chocolate, chopped
25g / 1oz / 2 tbsp unsalted butter

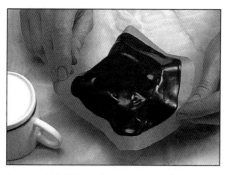

1 Make the chocolate cups. Cut out six 15 cm/6 in rounds of non-stick baking paper. Melt the chocolate with the butter in a heatproof bowl over a saucepan of simmering water. Stir until smooth, then spread a spoonful of the chocolate mixture over each circle, to within 2 cm/¾ in of the edge.

2 Carefully lift each paper round and drape it over an upturned teacup or ramekin so that the edges curve into frills. Leave until completely set, then carefully lift off and peel away the paper to reveal the chocolate cups.

3 Make the filling. Using a hand-held electric mixer, beat the egg yolk and sugar in a bowl until smooth, then stir in the vanilla essence. Soften the mascarpone if necessary, then stir it into the egg yolk mixture. Beat until smooth.

4 In a separate bowl, mix the coffee, cocoa and liqueur. Break up the biscuits roughly, then stir them into the mixture.

5 Place the chocolate cups on individual plates. Divide half the biscuit mixture among them, then spoon over half the mascarpone mixture.

6 Spoon over the remaining biscuit mixture (including any free liquid), top with the rest of the mascarpone mixture and dust lightly with cocoa powder. Chill for about 30 minutes before serving.

WHITE CHOCOLATE PARFAIT

SERVES 10

225g/8oz white chocolate, chopped into
small pieces
600ml/1 pint/2½ cups whipping cream
120ml/4fl oz/½ cup milk
10 egg yolks
15ml/1 tbsp caster sugar
40g/1½oz/½ cup desiccated coconut
120ml/4fl oz/½ cup canned sweetened
coconut milk
150g/5oz/1¼ cups unsalted macadamia nuts
curls of fresh coconut, to decorate
FOR THE CHOCOLATE ICING
225g/8oz plain chocolate, chopped into
small pieces
75g/3oz/6 tbsp butter
20ml/generous 1 tbsp golden syrup
175ml/6fl oz/¾ cup whipping cream

1 Carefully line the base and sides of a 1.4 litre/2⅓ pint/6 cup terrine mould or loaf tin with clear film.

2 Melt the chopped white chocolate with 50ml/2fl oz/¼ cup of the cream in the top of a double boiler or a heatproof bowl set over a saucepan of simmering water. Stir continually until the mixture is smooth. Set aside.

3 Put the milk in a pan. Add 250ml/ 8fl oz/1 cup of the remaining cream and bring to boiling point over a medium heat stirring constantly.

4 Meanwhile, whisk the egg yolks and caster sugar together in a large bowl, until thick and pale.

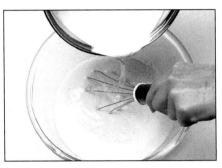

5 Add the hot cream mixture to the yolks, whisking constantly. Pour back into the saucepan and cook over a low heat for 2–3 minutes, until thickened. Stir constantly and do not boil. Remove the pan from the heat.

6 Add the melted chocolate, desiccated coconut and coconut milk, then stir well and leave to cool. Whip the remaining cream in a bowl until thick, then fold into the chocolate and coconut mixture.

7 Put 475ml/16fl oz/2 cups of the parfait mixture in the prepared mould or tin and spread evenly. Cover and freeze for about 2 hours, until just firm. Cover the remaining mixture and chill.

VARIATION

White Chocolate and Ginger Parfait: Use sliced stem ginger instead of macadamia nuts for the central layer of the parfait, and substitute syrup from the jar of ginger for the golden syrup in the icing. Leave out the coconut, if you prefer, and use sweetened condensed milk instead of the coconut milk.

8 Scatter the macadamia nuts evenly over the frozen parfait. Spoon in the remaining parfait mixture and level the surface. Cover the terrine and freeze for 6–8 hours or overnight, until the parfait is firm.

9 To make the icing, melt the chocolate with the butter and syrup in the top of a double boiler set over hot water. Stir occasionally.

10 Heat the cream in a saucepan, until just simmering, then stir into the chocolate mixture. Remove the pan from the heat and leave the mixture to cool until lukewarm.

11 To turn out the parfait, wrap the terrine or tin in a hot towel and set it upside down on a plate. Lift off the terrine or tin, then peel off the clear film. Place the parfait on a rack over a baking sheet and pour the icing evenly over the top. Working quickly, smooth the icing down the sides with a palette knife. Leave to set slightly, then transfer to a freezer-proof plate and freeze for 3–4 hours more.

12 Remove from the freezer about 15 minutes before serving, to allow the ice cream to soften slightly. When ready to serve, cut into slices, using a knife dipped in hot water between each slice. Serve, decorated with coconut curls.

CHOCOLATE AND CHESTNUT POTS

SERVES 6

250g/9oz plain chocolate
60ml/4 tbsp Madeira
25g/1oz/2 tbsp butter, diced
2 eggs, separated
225g/8oz/1 cup unsweetened chestnut purée
crème fraîche and chocolate curls, to decorate

1 Make a few chocolate curls for decoration, then break the rest of the chocolate into squares and melt it with the Madeira in a heatproof bowl over a saucepan of barely simmering water. Remove from the heat and add the butter, a few pieces at a time, stirring until melted and smooth.

2 Beat the egg yolks quickly into the mixture, then beat in the chestnut purée, a little at a time, making sure that each addition is absorbed before you add the next, mixing until smooth.

3 Whisk the egg whites in a clean, grease-free bowl until stiff. Stir about 15ml/1 tbsp of the whites into the chestnut mixture to lighten it, then fold in the rest evenly.

4 Spoon the mixture into six small ramekin dishes or custard cups and chill until set. Serve the pots topped with a generous spoonful of crème fraîche or whipped double cream. Decorate with the chocolate curls.

MOCHA VELVET CREAM POTS

SERVES 8

15ml/1 tbsp instant coffee powder
475ml/16fl oz/2 cups milk
75g/3oz/6 tbsp caster sugar
225g/8oz plain chocolate, chopped into small pieces
10ml/2 tsp vanilla essence
30ml/2 tbsp coffee liqueur (optional)
7 egg yolks
whipped cream and crystallized mimosa balls, to decorate

1 Preheat oven to 160°C/325°F/Gas 3. Place eight 120ml/ 4fl oz/½ cup custard cups or ramekins in a roasting tin. Set the tin aside.

2 Put the instant coffee into a saucepan. Stir in the milk, then add the sugar and set the pan over a medium heat. Bring to the boil, stirring constantly, until both the coffee and the sugar have dissolved completely.

3 Remove the pan from the heat and add the chocolate. Stir until it has melted and the sauce is smooth. Stir in the vanilla essence and coffee liqueur, if using.

4 In a bowl, whisk the egg yolks to blend them lightly. Slowly whisk in the chocolate mixture until well mixed, then strain the mixture into a large jug and divide equally among the cups or ramekins. Pour enough boiling water into the roasting tin to come halfway up the sides of the cups or ramekins. Carefully place the roasting tin in the oven.

5 Bake for 30–35 minutes, until the custard is just set and a knife inserted into the custard comes out clean. Remove the cups or ramekins from the roasting tin and allow to cool. Place on a baking sheet, cover and chill completely. Decorate with whipped cream and crystallized mimosa balls, if desired.

CHOCOLATE PAVLOVA WITH PASSION FRUIT CREAM

SERVES 6

4 egg whites
200g / 7oz / scant 1 cup caster sugar
20ml / 4 tsp cornflour
45ml / 3 tbsp cocoa powder
5ml / 1 tsp vinegar
chocolate leaves, to decorate

FOR THE FILLING

150g / 5oz plain chocolate, chopped into
small pieces
250ml / 8fl oz / 1 cup double cream
150g / 5oz / ⅔ cup Greek-style yogurt
2.5ml / ½ tsp vanilla essence
4 passion fruit

1 Preheat oven to 140°C/275°F/Gas 1. Cut a piece of non-stick baking paper to fit a baking sheet. Draw a 23 cm/9 in circle on the paper.

2 Whisk the egg whites in a clean, grease-free bowl until stiff. Gradually whisk in the sugar and continue to whisk until the mixture is stiff again. Whisk in the cornflour, cocoa and vinegar.

3 Place the baking paper upside down on the baking sheet. Spread the mixture over the marked circle, making a slight dip in the centre. Bake for 1½–2 hours.

4 Make the filling. Melt the chocolate in a heatproof bowl over barely simmering water, then remove from the heat and cool slightly. In a separate bowl, whip the cream with the yogurt and vanilla essence until thick. Fold 60ml/4 tbsp into the chocolate, then set both mixtures aside.

5 Halve all the passion fruit and scoop out the pulp. Stir half into the plain cream mixture. Carefully remove the meringue shell from the baking sheet and place it on a large serving plate. Fill with the passion fruit cream, then spoon over the chocolate mixture and the remaining passion fruit pulp.

6 Decorate with chocolate leaves and serve as soon as possible, while the meringue is still crisp on the outside and deliciously chewy within.

CHOCOLATE SORBET

SERVES 6

150g / 5oz bittersweet chocolate, chopped
115g / 4oz plain chocolate, grated
225g / 8oz / 1¼ cups caster sugar
475ml / 16fl oz / 2 cups water
chocolate curls, to decorate

1 Put all the chocolate in a food processor, fitted with the metal blade, and process for 20–30 seconds until finely chopped.
2 In a saucepan over a medium heat, bring the sugar and water to the boil, stirring until the sugar dissolves. Boil for about 2 minutes, then remove the pan from the heat.
3 With the machine running, pour the hot syrup over the chocolate in the food processor. Keep the machine running for 1–2 minutes until the chocolate is completely melted and the mixture is smooth, scraping down the bowl once.
4 Strain the chocolate mixture into a large measuring jug or bowl. Leave to cool, then chill, stirring occasionally. Freeze the mixture in an ice-cream maker. Alternatively, pour into a container suitable for use in the freezer, freeze until slushy, whisk until smooth, then freeze again. Whisk for a second time before the mixture hardens completely. Allow the sorbet to soften for 5–10 minutes at room temperature and serve in scoops, decorated with chocolate curls.

CHOCOLATE SORBET WITH RED FRUITS

SERVES 6

475ml / 16fl oz / 2 cups water
45ml / 3 tbsp clear honey
115g / 4oz / ½ cup caster sugar
75g / 3oz / ¾ cup cocoa powder
50g / 2oz plain dark or bittersweet chocolate, chopped into
small pieces
400g / 14oz soft red fruits, such as raspberries, redcurrants
or strawberries

1 Place the water, honey, caster sugar and cocoa powder in a saucepan. Heat gently, stirring occasionally, until the sugar has completely dissolved.
2 Remove the pan from the heat, add the chocolate and stir until melted. Leave until cool.
3 Tip into an ice-cream maker and churn until frozen. Alternatively, pour into a container suitable for use in the freezer, freeze until slushy, whisk until smooth, then freeze again. Whisk for a second time before the mixture hardens completely, and cover the container.
4 Remove from the freezer 10–15 minutes before serving, so that the sorbet softens slightly. Serve in scoops in chilled dessert bowls, with the soft fruits.

CHOCOLATE MINT ICE CREAM PIE

SERVES 8

75g / 3 oz plain chocolate chips
40g / 1½oz butter or margarine
50g / 2oz crisped rice cereal
1 litre / 1¾ pints / 4 cups mint-chocolate-chip
ice cream
chocolate curls, to decorate

1 Line a 23 cm/9 in pie tin with foil. Place a round of greaseproof paper over the foil in the bottom of the tin.
2 In a heatproof bowl set over a saucepan of simmering water melt the chocolate chips with the butter or margarine.
3 Remove the bowl from the heat and gently stir in the cereal, a little at a time.

4 Press the chocolate-cereal mixture evenly over the base and up the sides of the prepared tin, forming a 1 cm/½ in rim. Chill until completely hard.
5 Carefully remove the cereal base from the tin and peel off the foil and paper. Return the base to the pie tin.

6 Remove the ice cream from the freezer and allow it to soften for 10 minutes.

7 Spread the ice cream evenly in the biscuit case crust. Freeze until firm.
8 Scatter the chocolate curls over the ice cream just before serving.

ICE CREAM BOMBES

SERVES 6

*1 litre / 1¾ pints / 4 cups soft-scoop chocolate
ice cream*

*475ml / 16fl oz / 2 cups soft-scoop vanilla
ice cream*

50g / 2oz / ⅓ cup plain chocolate chips

115g / 4oz toffees

75ml / 5 tbsp double cream

1 Divide the chocolate ice cream equally among six small cups. Push it roughly to the base and up the sides, leaving a small cup-shaped dip in the middle. Return to the freezer and leave for 45 minutes. Take the cups out again and smooth the ice cream in each into shape, keeping the centre hollow. Return to the freezer.

2 Put the vanilla ice cream in a small bowl and break it up slightly with a spoon. Stir in the chocolate chips and use this mixture to fill the hollows in the cups of chocolate ice cream. Smooth the tops, then cover the cups with clear film, return to the freezer and leave overnight.

3 Melt the toffees with the cream in a small pan over a very low heat, stirring constantly until smooth, warm and creamy.

4 Turn out the bombes on to individual plates and pour the toffee sauce over the top. Serve immediately.

CHOCOLATE FUDGE SUNDAES

SERVES 4

4 scoops each vanilla and coffee ice cream
2 small ripe bananas
whipped cream
toasted flaked almonds
FOR THE SAUCE
50g/2oz/⅓ cup soft light brown sugar
120ml/4fl oz/½ cup golden syrup
45ml/3 tbsp strong black coffee
5ml/1 tsp ground cinnamon
150g/5oz plain chocolate, chopped into
small pieces
75ml/3fl oz/5 tbsp whipping cream
45ml/3 tbsp coffee-flavoured liqueur
(optional)

1 Make the sauce. Place the sugar, syrup, coffee and cinnamon in a heavy-based saucepan. Bring to the boil, then boil for about 5 minutes, stirring the mixture constantly.

2 Turn off the heat and stir in the chocolate. When the chocolate has melted and the mixture is smooth, stir in the cream and the liqueur, if using. Leave the sauce to cool slightly. If made ahead, reheat the sauce gently until just warm.

3 Fill four glasses with a scoop each of vanilla and coffee ice cream.

4 Peel the bananas and slice them thinly. Scatter the sliced bananas over the ice cream. Pour the warm fudge sauce over the bananas, then top each sundae with a generous swirl of whipped cream. Sprinkle the sundaes with toasted almonds and serve at once.

CHOCOLATE ICE CREAM

SERVES 4–6

750ml / 1¼ pints / 3 cups milk
10 cm / 4 in piece of vanilla pod
4 egg yolks
115g / 4oz / ½ cup granulated sugar
225g / 8oz plain chocolate, chopped into
small pieces

<u>1</u> Heat the milk with the vanilla pod in a small saucepan. Remove from the heat as soon as small bubbles start to form on the surface. Do not let it boil. Strain the milk into a jug and set aside.

<u>2</u> Using a wire whisk or hand-held electric mixer, beat the egg yolks in a bowl. Gradually whisk in the sugar and continue to whisk until the mixture is pale and thick. Slowly add the milk to the egg mixture, whisking after each addition. When all the milk has been added, pour the mixture into a heatproof bowl.

<u>3</u> Place the heatproof bowl over a saucepan of simmering water and add the chocolate. Stir over a low heat until the chocolate melts, then raise the heat slightly and continue to stir the chocolate-flavoured custard until it thickens enough to coat the back of a wooden spoon lightly. Remove the custard from the heat, pour into a bowl and allow to cool, stirring occasionally to prevent skin forming on the surface.

<u>4</u> Freeze the chocolate mixture in an ice-cream maker, following the manufacturer's instructions, or pour it into a suitable container for freezing. Freeze for about 3 hours, or until set. Remove from the container and chop roughly into 7.5 cm / 3 in pieces. Place in a food processor and chop until smooth. Return to the freezer container and freeze again. Repeat two or three times, until the ice cream is smooth and creamy.

ROCKY ROAD ICE CREAM

SERVES 6

115g/4oz plain chocolate, chopped into
small pieces
150ml/¼ pint/⅔ cup milk
300ml/½ pint/1¼ cups double cream
115g/4oz/2 cups marshmallows, chopped
115g/4oz/½ cup glacé cherries, chopped
50g/2oz/½ cup crumbled shortbread biscuits
30ml/2 tbsp chopped walnuts

1 Melt the chocolate in the milk in a saucepan over a gentle heat, stirring from time to time. Pour into a bowl and leave to cool completely.

2 Whip the cream in a separate bowl until it just holds its shape. Beat in the chocolate mixture, a little at a time, until the mixture is smooth and creamy.

3 Tip the mixture into an ice-cream maker and, following the manufacturer's instructions, churn until almost frozen. Alternatively, pour into a container suitable for use in the freezer, freeze until ice crystals form around the edges, then whisk with a strong hand whisk or hand-held electric mixer until smooth.

4 Stir the marshmallows, glacé cherries, crushed biscuits and nuts into the iced mixture, then return to the freezer container and freeze until firm.

5 Allow the ice cream to soften at room temperature for 15–20 minutes before serving in scoops. Add a wafer and chocolate sauce to each portion, if desired.

LITTLE CAKES,
BISCUITS & BARS

CHUNKY CHOCOLATE BARS

MAKES 12

350g / 12oz plain chocolate, chopped into
small pieces
115g / 4oz / ½ cup unsalted butter
400g / 14oz can condensed milk
225g / 8oz digestive biscuits, broken
50g / 2oz / ⅓ cup raisins
115g / 4oz ready-to-eat dried peaches,
roughly chopped
50g / 2oz / ½ cup hazelnuts or pecan nuts,
roughly chopped

1 Line a 28 x 18 cm / 11 x 7 in cake tin with clear film.
2 Melt the chocolate and butter in a large heatproof bowl over a pan of simmering water. Stir until well mixed.

3 Pour the condensed milk into the chocolate and butter mixture. Beat with a wooden spoon until creamy.
4 Add the broken biscuits, raisins, chopped peaches and hazelnuts or pecans. Mix well until all the ingredients are coated in the rich chocolate sauce.

5 Tip the mixture into the prepared tin, making sure it is pressed well into the corners. Leave the top craggy. Cool, then chill until set.
6 Lift the cake out of the tin using the clear film and then peel off the film. Cut into 12 bars and serve at once.

CHOCOLATE LEMON TARTLETS

MAKES 12 TARTLETS
450g / 1lb Shortcrust Pastry
lemon twists and melted chocolate to decorate
FOR THE LEMON CUSTARD SAUCE
grated rind and juice of 1 lemon
350ml / 12fl oz / 1½ cups milk
6 egg yolks
50g / 2oz / ½ cup caster sugar
FOR THE LEMON CURD FILLING
grated rind and juice of 2 lemons
175g / 6oz / ¾ cup unsalted butter, diced
450g / 1lb / 2 cups granulated sugar
3 eggs, lightly beaten
FOR THE CHOCOLATE LAYER
175ml / 6fl oz / ¾ cup double cream
175g / 6oz bittersweet or plain chocolate,
chopped into small pieces
25g / 1oz / 2 tbsp unsalted butter, cut into
pieces

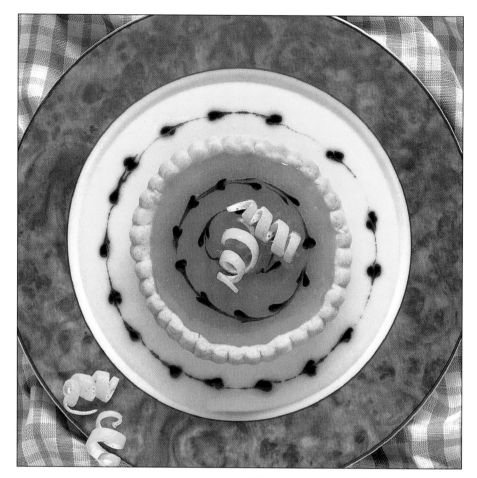

1 Prepare the custard sauce. Place the rind in a saucepan with the milk. Bring to the boil over a medium heat. Remove from the heat and allow to stand for 5 minutes to infuse. Strain the milk into a clean pan and reheat it gently.
2 In a bowl beat the yolks and sugar with a hand-held electric mixer for 2–3 minutes, until pale and thick. Pour over about 250ml / 8fl oz / 1 cup of the flavoured hot milk, beating vigorously.
3 Return the yolk mixture to the rest of the milk in the pan and cook gently, stirring constantly, over low heat until the mixture thickens and lightly coats the back of a spoon. (Do not allow sauce to boil or it will curdle.) Strain into a chilled bowl. Stir 30ml / 2 tbsp lemon juice into the sauce. Cool, stirring occasionally, then chill until ready to use.
4 Prepare the lemon curd filling. Combine the lemon rind, juice, butter and sugar in the top of a double boiler. Set over simmering water and heat gently until the butter has melted and the sugar has completely dissolved. Reduce the heat to low.
5 Stir the lightly beaten eggs into the butter mixture. Cook over a low heat, for 15 minutes, stirring constantly, until the mixture coats the back of a spoon.

6 Strain the lemon curd into a bowl and cover closely with clear film. Allow to cool, stirring occasionally, then chill to thicken, stirring occasionally.
7 Lightly butter twelve 7.5 cm / 3 in tartlet tins (if possible ones which have removable bases). On a lightly floured surface, roll out the pastry to a thickness of 3 mm / ⅛ in. Using a 10 cm / 4 in fluted cutter, cut out 12 rounds and press each one into a tartlet tin. Prick the bases with a fork. Place the tins on a baking sheet and chill for 30 minutes.

8 Preheat oven to 190°C / 375°F / Gas 5. Cut out rounds of foil and line each pastry case; fill with baking beans or rice. Bake blind for 5–8 minutes. Remove the foil with the beans and bake for 5 more minutes, until the cases are golden. Remove to rack to cool.
9 Prepare the chocolate layer. In a saucepan over a medium heat, bring the cream to the boil. Remove from the heat and add the chocolate all at once; stir until melted. Beat in the butter and cool slightly. Pour the filling into each tartlet to make a layer 5 mm / ¼ in thick. Chill for 10 minutes until set.
10 Remove the tartlets from the tins and spoon in a layer of lemon curd to come to the top of the pastry. Set aside, but do not chill. To serve, spoon a little lemon custard sauce on to a plate and place a tartlet in the centre. Decorate with a lemon twist. Dot the custard with melted chocolate. Draw a skewer through the chocolate to make heart motifs.

CHOCOLATE-DIPPED HAZELNUT CRESCENTS

MAKES ABOUT 35

275g / 10oz / 2 cups plain flour
pinch of salt
225g / 8oz / 1 cup unsalted butter, softened
75g / 3oz / 6 tbsp caster sugar
15ml / 1 tbsp hazelnut-flavoured liqueur
or water
5ml / 1 tsp vanilla essence
75g / 3oz plain chocolate, chopped into
small pieces
50g / 2oz / ½ cup hazelnuts, toasted and
finely chopped
icing sugar, for dusting
350g / 12oz plain chocolate, melted, for
dipping

1 Preheat oven to 160°C/325°F/Gas 3. Grease two large baking sheets. Sift the flour and salt into a bowl. In a separate bowl, beat the butter until creamy. Add the sugar and beat until fluffy, then beat in the hazelnut liqueur or water and the vanilla essence. Gently stir in the flour mixture, then the chocolate and hazelnuts.
2 With floured hands, shape the dough into 5 x 1 cm/2 x ½ in crescent shapes. Place on the baking sheets, 5 cm/2 in apart. Bake for 20–25 minutes until the edges are set and the biscuits slightly golden. Remove the biscuits from the oven and cool on the baking sheets for 10 minutes, then transfer the biscuits to wire racks to cool completely.

3 Have the melted chocolate ready in a small bowl. Dust the biscuits lightly with icing sugar. Using a pair of kitchen tongs or your fingers, dip half of each crescent into the melted chocolate. Place the crescents on a non-stick baking sheet until the chocolate has set.

Brioches au Chocolat

Makes 12

250g / 9oz / 2¼ cups strong white flour
pinch of salt
30ml / 2 tbsp caster sugar
1 sachet easy-blend dried yeast
3 eggs, beaten, plus extra beaten egg,
for glazing
45ml / 3 tbsp hand-hot milk
115g / 4oz / ½ cup unsalted butter, diced
175g / 6oz plain chocolate, broken into
squares

1 Sift the flour and salt into a large mixing bowl and stir in the sugar and yeast. Make a well in the centre of the mixture and add the eggs and milk.

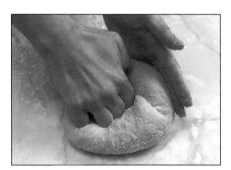

2 Beat the egg and milk mixture well, gradually incorporating the surrounding dry ingredients to make a fairly soft dough. Turn the dough on to a lightly floured surface and knead well for about 5 minutes, until smooth and elastic, adding a little more flour if necessary.
3 Add the butter to the dough, a few pieces at a time, kneading until each addition is absorbed before adding the next. When all the butter has been incorporated and small bubbles appear in the dough, wrap it in clear film and chill for at least 1 hour. If you intend serving the brioches for breakfast, the dough can be left overnight.

4 Lightly grease 12 individual brioche tins set on a baking sheet or a 12-hole brioche or patty tin. Divide the brioche dough into 12 pieces and shape each into a smooth round. Place a chocolate square in the centre of each round. Bring up the sides of the dough and press the edges firmly together to seal, use a little beaten egg if necessary.
5 Place the brioches, join side down, in the prepared tins. Cover and leave them in a warm place for about 30 minutes or until doubled in size. Preheat oven to 200°C/400°F/Gas 6.

6 Brush the brioches with beaten egg. Bake for 12–15 minutes, until well risen and golden brown. Place on wire racks and leave until they have cooled slightly. They should be served warm and can be made in advance and reheated if necessary. Do not serve straight from the oven, as the chocolate will be very hot.

Cook's Tip
Brioches freeze well for up to 1 month. Thaw at room temperature, then reheat on baking sheets in a low oven and serve warm, but not hot. For a richer variation serve with melted chocolate drizzled over the top of the brioches.

CHOCOLATE AND TOFFEE BARS

MAKES 32

350g/12oz/2 cups soft light brown sugar
450g/1lb/2 cups butter or margarine, at room temperature
2 egg yolks
7.5ml/1½ tsp vanilla essence
450g/1lb/4 cups plain or wholemeal flour
2.5ml/½ tsp salt
175g/6oz plain chocolate, broken into squares
115g/4oz/1 cup walnuts or pecan nuts, chopped

1 Preheat oven to 180°C/350°F/Gas 4. Beat the sugar and butter or margarine in a mixing bowl until light and fluffy. Beat in the egg yolks and vanilla essence, then stir in the flour and salt to make a soft dough.

2 Spread the dough in a greased 33 x 23 x 5 cm/13 x 9 x 2 in baking tin. Level the surface. Bake for 25–30 minutes, until lightly browned. The texture will be soft.

3 Remove the bake from the oven and immediately place the chocolate on top. Set aside until the chocolate is soft, then spread it out with a spatula. Sprinkle with the chopped nuts.

4 While the bake is still warm, cut it into 5 x 4 cm/2 x 1½ in bars, remove from the tin and leave to cool on a wire rack.

CHOCOLATE PECAN SQUARES

MAKES 16

2 eggs
10ml/2 tsp vanilla essence
pinch of salt
175g/6oz/1½ cups pecan nuts, roughly chopped
50g/2oz/½ cup plain flour
50g/2oz/¼ cup granulated sugar
120ml/4fl oz/½ cup golden syrup
75g/3oz plain chocolate, chopped into small pieces
40g/1½oz/3 tbsp unsalted butter
16 pecan nut halves, to decorate

1 Preheat oven to 160°C/325°F/Gas 3. Line a 20 cm/8 in square baking tin with non-stick baking paper.

2 In a bowl, whisk the eggs with the vanilla essence and salt. In another bowl, mix together the pecan nuts and flour.

3 Put the sugar in a saucepan, add the golden syrup and bring to the boil. Remove from the heat and stir in the chocolate and butter with a wooden spoon until both have dissolved and the mixture is smooth. Stir in the beaten egg mixture, then fold in the pecan nuts and flour.

4 Pour the mixture into the prepared tin and bake for about 35 minutes or until firm to the touch. Cool in the tin for 10 minutes before turning out on a wire rack. Cut into 5 cm/2 in squares and press pecan halves into the tops while still warm. Cool completely before serving.

WHITE CHOCOLATE BROWNIES WITH MILK CHOCOLATE MACADAMIA TOPPING

SERVES 12

115g/4oz/1 cup plain flour
2.5ml/½ tsp baking powder
pinch of salt
175g/6oz fine quality white chocolate, chopped into small pieces
115g/4oz/½ cup caster sugar
115g/4oz/½ cup unsalted butter, cut into small pieces
2 eggs, lightly beaten
5ml/1 tsp vanilla essence
175g/6oz plain chocolate chips or plain chocolate, chopped into small pieces

FOR THE TOPPING

200g/7oz milk chocolate, chopped into small pieces
175g/6oz/1½ cups unsalted macadamia nuts, chopped

<u>1</u> Preheat oven to 180°C/350°F/Gas 4. Grease a 23 cm/9 in springform tin. Sift together the flour, baking powder and salt, set aside.

<u>2</u> In a medium saucepan over a low heat, melt the white chocolate, sugar and butter until smooth, stirring frequently. Cool slightly, then beat in the eggs and vanilla essence. Stir in the flour mixture until well blended. Stir in the chocolate chips or chopped chocolate. Spread evenly in the prepared tin.

<u>3</u> Bake for 20–25 minutes, until a cake tester inserted in the cake tin comes out clean; do not over-bake. Remove the cake from the oven and place the tin on a heatproof surface.

<u>4</u> Sprinkle the chopped milk chocolate evenly over the cake and return it to the oven for 1 minute.

<u>5</u> Remove the cake from the oven again and gently spread the softened chocolate evenly over the top. Sprinkle with the macadamia nuts and gently press them into the chocolate. Cool on a wire rack for 30 minutes, then chill, for about 1 hour, until set. Run a sharp knife around the side of the tin to loosen, then unclip the side of the springform tin and remove it carefully. Cut into thin wedges.

CHUNKY DOUBLE CHOCOLATE COOKIES

MAKES 18–20

115g/4oz/½ cup unsalted butter, softened
115g/4oz/⅔ cup light muscovado sugar
1 egg
5ml/1 tsp vanilla essence
150g/5oz/1¼ cups self-raising flour
75g/3oz/¾ cup porridge oats
115g/4oz plain chocolate, roughly chopped
115g/4oz white chocolate, roughly chopped

DOUBLE-CHOC ALMOND COOKIES:

Instead of the porridge oats, use 75g/3oz/¾ cup ground almonds. Omit the chopped chocolate and use 175g/6oz/1 cup chocolate chips instead. Top each heap of cake mixture with half a glacé cherry before baking.

1 Preheat oven to 190°C/375°F/Gas 5. Lightly grease two baking sheets. Cream the butter with the sugar in a bowl until pale and fluffy. Add the egg and vanilla essence and beat well.

2 Sift the flour over the mixture and fold in lightly with a metal spoon, then add the oats and chopped plain and white chocolate and stir until evenly mixed.

3 Place small spoonfuls of the mixture in 18–20 rocky heaps on the baking sheets, leaving space for spreading.

4 Bake for 12–15 minutes or until the biscuits are beginning to turn pale golden. Cool for 2–3 minutes on the baking sheets, then lift on to wire racks. The biscuits will be soft when freshly baked but will harden on cooling.

CHOCOLATE KISSES

MAKES 24

*75g / 3oz dark plain chocolate, chopped into
small pieces*
*75g / 3oz white chocolate, chopped into small
pieces*
115g / 4oz / ½ cup butter, softened
115g / 4oz / ½ cup caster sugar
2 eggs
225g / 8oz / 2 cups plain flour
icing sugar, to decorate

<u>1</u> Melt the plain and white chocolates in
separate bowls and set both aside to cool.
<u>2</u> Beat the butter and caster sugar
together until pale and fluffy. Beat in the
eggs, one at a time. Then sift in the flour
and mix well.

<u>3</u> Halve the creamed mixture and divide
it between the two bowls of chocolate.
Mix each chocolate in thoroughly so that
each forms a dough. Knead the doughs
until smooth, wrap them separately in
clear film and chill for 1 hour. Preheat
oven to 190°C/375°F/Gas 5.

<u>4</u> Shape slightly rounded teaspoonfuls of
both doughs roughly into balls. Roll the
balls between your palms to neaten them.
Arrange the balls on greased baking
sheets and bake for 10–12 minutes. Dust
liberally with sifted icing sugar and cool
on a wire rack.

CHOCOLATE CINNAMON TUILES

3 In a separate bowl, mix together the cocoa and cinnamon. Stir into the larger quantity of mixture until well combined. Leaving room for spreading, drop spoonfuls of the chocolate-flavoured mixture on to the prepared baking sheets, then spread each gently with a palette knife to make a neat round.

4 Using a small spoon, drizzle the reserved plain mixture over the rounds, swirling it lightly to give a marbled effect.

5 Bake for 4–6 minutes, until just set. Using a palette knife, lift each biscuit and drape it over a rolling pin, to give a curved shape as it hardens. Allow the tuiles to set, then remove them and finish cooling on a wire rack. Serve on the same day.

MAKES 12
1 egg white
50g/2oz/¼ cup caster sugar
30ml/2 tbsp plain flour
40g/1½oz/3 tbsp butter, melted
15ml/1 tbsp cocoa powder
2.5m/½ tsp ground cinnamon

1 Preheat oven to 200°C/400°F/Gas 6. Lightly grease two large baking sheets. Whisk the egg white in a clean, grease-free bowl until it forms soft peaks. Gradually whisk in the sugar to make a smooth, glossy mixture.

2 Sift the flour over the meringue mixture and fold in evenly; try not to deflate the mixture. Stir in the butter. Transfer about 45ml/3 tbsp of the mixture to a small bowl and set it aside.

CHOCOLATE CUPS
Cream 150g/5oz/⅔ cup butter with 115g/4oz/½ cup caster sugar. Stir in 75g/3oz/1 cup porridge oats, 15ml/1 tbsp cocoa powder and 5ml/1 tsp vanilla essence. Roll to the size of golf balls and space well on greased baking sheets. Bake at 180°C/350°F/Gas 4 for 12–15 minutes. Cool slightly then drape over greased upturned glasses until cool and firm. Makes 8–10.

CHOCOLATE MARZIPAN COOKIES

MAKES ABOUT 36

200g/7oz/scant 1 cup unsalted butter, softened
200g/7oz/generous 1 cup light muscovado sugar
1 egg, beaten
300g/11oz/2¾ cups plain flour
60ml/4 tbsp cocoa powder
200g/7oz white almond paste
115g/4oz white chocolate, chopped into small pieces

1 Preheat oven to 190°C/375°F/Gas 5. Lightly grease two large baking sheets. Using a hand-held electric mixer, cream the butter with the sugar in a mixing bowl until pale and fluffy. Add the egg and beat well.

2 Sift the flour and cocoa over the mixture. Stir in with a wooden spoon until all the flour mixture has been smoothly incorporated, then use clean hands to press the mixture together to make a fairly soft dough.

3 Using a rolling pin and keeping your touch light, roll out about half the dough on a lightly floured surface to a thickness of about 5 mm/¼ in. Using a 5 cm/2 in plain or fluted biscuit cutter, cut out 36 rounds, re-rolling the dough as required. Wrap the remaining dough in clear film and set it aside.

4 Cut the almond paste into 36 equal pieces. Roll into balls, flatten slightly and place one on each round of dough. Roll out the remaining dough, cut out more rounds, then place on top of the almond paste. Press the dough edges to seal.

5 Bake for 10–12 minutes, or until the cookies have risen well and are beginning to crack on the surface. Cool on the baking sheet for about 2–3 minutes, then finish cooling on a wire rack.

6 Melt the white chocolate, then either drizzle it over the biscuits to decorate, or spoon into a paper piping bag and quickly pipe a design on to the biscuits.

VARIATION
Use glacé icing instead of melted white chocolate to decorate the cookies, if you prefer.

SWEETS & TRUFFLES

DOUBLE CHOCOLATE-DIPPED FRUIT

MAKES 24 COATED PIECES

fruits – about 24 pieces (strawberries, cherries, orange segments, large seedless grapes, physalis (Cape gooseberries), kumquats, stoned prunes, stoned dates, dried apricots, dried peaches or dried pears)
115g/4oz white chocolate, chopped into small pieces
115g/4oz bittersweet or plain chocolate, chopped into small pieces

1 Clean and prepare fruits; wipe strawberries with a soft cloth or brush gently with pastry brush. Wash firm-skinned fruits such as cherries and grapes and dry well. Peel and leave whole or cut up any other fruits being used.

CHOCOLATE PEPPERMINT CREAMS

1 egg white
90ml/6 tbsp double cream
5ml/1 tsp peppermint essence
675g/1½lb/5½ cups icing sugar, plus extra for dusting
few drops of green food colouring
175g/6oz plain chocolate, chopped into small pieces

1 Beat the egg white lightly in a bowl. Mix in the cream and peppermint essence, then gradually add the icing sugar to make a firm, pliable dough. Work in 1–2 drops of green food colouring (apply it from a cocktail stick if you are anxious about adding too much colour) until the dough is an even, pale green.
2 On a surface dusted with icing sugar, roll out the dough to a thickness of about 1cm/½in. Stamp out 4cm/1½in rounds of squares and place on a baking sheet lined with non-stick baking paper. Leave to dry for at least 8 hours, turning once.
3 Melt the chocolate in a bowl over barely simmering water. Allow to cool slightly. Spread chocolate over the top of each peppermint cream, and place them on fresh sheets of non-stick paper. Chill until set.

2 Melt the white chocolate. Remove from the heat and cool to tepid (about 29°C/84°F), stirring frequently. Line a baking sheet with non-stick baking paper. Holding each fruit by the stem or end and at an angle, dip about two-thirds of the fruit into the chocolate. Allow the excess to drip off and place on the baking sheet. Chill the fruits for about 20 minutes until the chocolate sets.

3 Melt the bittersweet or plain chocolate, stirring frequently until smooth.

4 Remove the chocolate from the heat and cool to just below body temperature, about 30°C/86°F. Take each white chocolate-coated fruit in turn from the baking sheet and, holding by the stem or end and at the opposite angle, dip the bottom third of each piece into the dark chocolate, creating a chevron effect. Set on the baking sheet. Chill for 15 minutes or until set. Before serving, allow the fruit to stand at room temperature 10–15 minutes before serving.

RICH CHOCOLATE PISTACHIO FUDGE

MAKES 36

250g/9oz/generous 1 cup granulated sugar
375g/13oz can sweetened condensed milk
50g/2oz/¼ cup unsalted butter
5ml/1 tsp vanilla essence
115g/4oz plain dark chocolate, grated
75g/3oz/¾ cup pistachio nuts, almonds or hazelnuts

**CHOCOLATE- AND
MARSHMALLOW FUDGE**

25g/1oz/2 tbsp butter
350g/12oz/1½ cups granulated sugar
175ml/6fl oz/¾ cup evaporated milk
pinch of salt
115g/4oz/2 cups white mini marshmallows
225g/8oz /1¼ cups chocolate chips
5ml/1 tsp vanilla essence
115g/4oz/½ cup chopped walnuts (optional)

<u>1</u> Generously grease an 18cm/7 in cake tin. Mix the butter, sugar, evaporated milk and salt in a heavy-based saucepan. Stir over a medium heat until the sugar has dissolved, then bring to the boil and cook for 3–5 minutes or until thickened, stirring all the time.

<u>2</u> Remove the pan from the heat and beat in the marshmallows and chocolate chips until dissolved. Beat in the vanilla essence. Scrape the mixture into the prepared cake tin and press it evenly into the corners, using a metal palette knife. Level the surface.

<u>3</u> If using the walnuts, sprinkle them over the fudge and press them in to the surface. Set the fudge aside to cool. Before it has set completely, mark it into squares with a sharp knife. Chill until firm before cutting the fudge up and serving it.

<u>1</u> Grease a 19cm/7½in square cake tin and line with non-stick baking paper. Mix the sugar, condensed milk and butter in a heavy-based pan. Heat gently, stirring occasionally, until the sugar has dissolved completely and the mixture is smooth.

<u>2</u> Bring the mixture to the boil, stirring occasionally, and boil until it registers 116°C/240°F on a sugar thermometer or until a small amount of the mixture dropped into a cup of iced water forms a soft ball.

<u>3</u> Remove the pan from the heat and beat in the vanilla essence, chocolate and nuts. Beat vigorously until the mixture is smooth and creamy.

<u>4</u> Pour the mixture into the prepared cake tin and spread evenly. Leave until just set, then mark into squares. Leave to set completely before cutting into squares and removing from the tin. Store in an airtight container in a cool place.

COGNAC AND GINGER CREAMS

MAKES 18–20

*300g / 11oz plain dark chocolate, chopped
into small pieces
45ml / 3 tbsp double cream
30ml / 2 tbsp cognac
4 pieces of stem ginger, finely chopped, plus
15ml / 1 tbsp syrup from the jar
crystallized ginger, to decorate*

<u>1</u> Polish the insides of 18–20 chocolate moulds carefully with cotton wool. Melt about two-thirds of the chocolate in a heatproof bowl over a saucepan of barely simmering water, then spoon a little into each mould. Reserve a little of the melted chocolate, for sealing the creams.

<u>2</u> Using a small brush, sweep the chocolate up the sides of the moulds to coat them evenly, then invert them on to a sheet of greaseproof paper and set aside until the chocolate has set.

CHOCOLATE MARSHMALLOW DIPS
Have ready a large baking sheet lined with non-stick baking paper. Melt 175g / 6oz plain or bittersweet chocolate in a heatproof bowl over barely simmering water. Stir until smooth. Remove the pan from the heat, but leave the bowl in place, so that the chocolate does not solidify too soon. You will need 15–20 large or 30–35 small marshmallows. Using cocktail sticks, spear each marshmallow and coat in the chocolate. Roll in ground hazelnuts. Place on the lined baking sheet and chill until set before removing the skewers. Place each marshmallow dip in a foil sweet case.

<u>3</u> Melt the remaining chopped chocolate over simmering water, then stir in the cream, cognac, stem ginger and ginger syrup, mixing well. Spoon into the chocolate-lined moulds. If the reserved chocolate has solidified, melt, then spoon a little into each mould to seal.

<u>4</u> Leave the chocolates in a cool place (not the fridge) until set. To remove them from the moulds, gently press them out on to a cool surface, such as a marble slab. Decorate with small pieces of crystallized ginger. Keep the chocolates cool if not serving them immediately.

CHOCOLATE-COATED NUT BRITTLE

MAKES 20–24 PIECES

*115g/4oz/1 cup mixed pecan nuts and whole
almonds
115g/4oz/½ cup caster sugar
60ml/4 tbsp water
200g/7oz plain dark chocolate, chopped into
small pieces*

<u>1</u> Lightly grease a baking sheet with
butter or oil. Mix the nuts, sugar and
water in a heavy-based saucepan. Place
the pan over a gentle heat, stirring until
all the sugar has dissolved.

<u>2</u> Bring to the boil, then lower the heat to
moderate and cook until the mixture
turns a rich golden brown and registers
155°C/310°F on a sugar thermometer. If
you do not have a sugar thermometer,
test the syrup by adding a few drops to a
cup of iced water. The mixture should
solidify to a very brittle mass.

CHOCOLATE-COATED HAZELNUTS

Roast about 225g/8oz/2 cups
hazelnuts in the oven or under the
grill. Allow to cool. Melt the
chocolate in a heatproof bowl over a
pan of barely simmering water.
Remove from the heat, but leave the
bowl over the water so that the
chocolate remains liquid. Have
ready about 30 paper sweet cases,
arranged on baking sheets. Add
the roasted hazelnuts to the
melted chocolate and stir to coat.
Using two spoons, carefully scoop
up a cluster of two or three
chocolate-coated nuts. Carefully
transfer the cluster to a paper sweet
case. Leave the nut clusters in a cool
place until set.

<u>3</u> Quickly remove the pan from the heat
and tip the mixture on to the prepared
baking sheet, spreading it evenly. Leave
until completely cold and hard.

<u>4</u> Break the nut brittle into bite-size
pieces. Melt the chocolate and dip the
pieces to half-coat them. Leave on a sheet
of non-stick baking paper to set.

TRUFFLE-FILLED FILO CUPS

MAKES ABOUT 24 CUPS

*3–6 sheets fresh or thawed frozen filo pastry,
depending on size*
40g / 1½ oz / 3 tbsp unsalted butter, melted
sugar, for sprinkling
pared strips of lemon zest, to decorate
**FOR THE CHOCOLATE TRUFFLE
MIXTURE**
250ml / 8fl oz / 1 cup double cream
*225g / 8oz bittersweet or plain chocolate,
chopped into small pieces*
*50g / 2oz / ¼ cup unsalted butter, cut into
small pieces*
30ml / 2 tbsp brandy or liqueur

<u>1</u> Prepare the truffle mixture. In a
saucepan over a medium heat, bring the
cream to a boil. Remove from the heat
and add the pieces of chocolate, stirring
until melted. Beat in the butter and add
the brandy or liqueur. Strain into a bowl
and chill for 1 hour until thick.

<u>2</u> Preheat oven to 200°C/400°F/Gas 6.
Grease a 12-hole bun tray. Cut the filo
sheets into 6cm/2½ in squares. Cover
with a damp dish towel. Place one square
on a work surface. Brush lightly with
melted butter, turn over and brush the
other side. Sprinkle with a pinch of sugar.
Butter another square and place it over
the first at an angle; sprinkle with sugar.
Butter a third square and place over the
first two, unevenly, so the corners form
an uneven edge. Press the layered square
into one of the holes in the bun tray.

<u>3</u> Continue to fill the tray, working
quickly so that the filo does not have time
to dry out. Bake the filo cups for 4–6
minutes, until golden. Cool for 10
minutes on the bun tray then carefully
transfer to a wire rack and cool
completely.

<u>4</u> Stir the chocolate mixture; it should be
just thick enough to pipe. Spoon the
mixture into a piping bag fitted with a
medium star nozzle and pipe a swirl into
each filo cup. Decorate each with tiny
strips of lemon zest.

CHOCOLATE TRUFFLES

**MAKES 20 LARGE OR 30 MEDIUM
TRUFFLES**

250ml / 8fl oz / 1 cup double cream
*275g / 10oz fine quality bittersweet or plain
chocolate, chopped into small pieces*
*40g / 1½oz / 3 tbsp unsalted butter, cut into
small pieces*
*45ml / 3 tbsp brandy, whisky or liqueur of
own choice*
cocoa powder, for dusting (optional)
*finely chopped pistachio nuts, to decorate
(optional)*
*400g / 14oz bittersweet chocolate, to decorate
(optional)*

1 Pour the cream into a saucepan. Bring to the boil over a medium heat. Remove from the heat and add the chocolate, all at once. Stir gently until melted. Stir in the butter until melted, then stir in the brandy, whisky or liqueur. Strain into a bowl and cool to room temperature. Cover the mixture with clear film and chill for 4 hours or overnight.

2 Line a large baking sheet with non-stick baking paper. Using a small ice cream scoop, melon baller or tablespoon, scrape up the mixture into 20 large balls or 30 medium balls and place on the lined baking sheet. Dip the scoop or spoon in cold water from time to time, to prevent the mixture from sticking.

3 If dusting with cocoa powder, sift a thick layer of cocoa on to a dish or pie plate. Roll the truffles in the cocoa, rounding them between the palms of your hands. (Dust your hands with cocoa to prevent the truffles from sticking.) Do not worry if the truffles are not perfectly round as an irregular shape looks more authentic. Alternatively, roll the truffles in very finely chopped pistachios. Chill on the paper-lined baking sheet until firm. Keep in the fridge for up to 10 days or freeze for up to 2 months.

4 If coating with chocolate, do not roll the truffles in cocoa, but freeze them for 1 hour. For perfect results, temper the chocolate. Alternatively, simply melt it in a heatproof bowl over a saucepan of barely simmering water. Using a fork, dip the truffles, one at a time, into the melted chocolate, tapping the fork on the edge of the bowl to shake off excess. Place on a baking sheet, lined with non-stick baking paper. If the chocolate begins to thicken, reheat it gently until smooth. Chill the truffles until set.

MALT WHISKY TRUFFLES

MAKES 25–30

200g/7oz plain dark chocolate, chopped into
small pieces
150ml/¼ pint/⅔ cup double cream
45ml/3 tbsp malt whisky
115g/4oz/¾ cup icing sugar
cocoa powder, for coating

1 Melt the chocolate in a heatproof bowl over a saucepan of simmering water, stir until smooth, then cool slightly.

2 Using a wire whisk, whip the cream with the whisky in a bowl until thick enough to hold its shape.

3 Stir in the melted chocolate and icing sugar, mixing evenly, then leave until firm enough to handle.

4 Dust your hands with cocoa powder and shape the mixture into bite-size balls. Coat in cocoa powder and pack into pretty cases or boxes. Store in the fridge for up to 3–4 days if necessary.

TRUFFLE-FILLED EASTER EGG

MAKES 1 LARGE, HOLLOW EASTER EGG

*350g/12oz plain couverture chocolate,
tempered, or plain, milk or white chocolate,
melted*
Chocolate Truffles

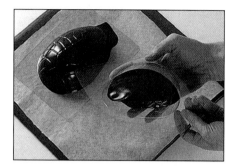

1 Line a small baking sheet with non-stick baking paper. Using a small ladle or spoon, pour in enough melted chocolate to coat both halves of an Easter egg mould. Tilt the half-moulds slowly to coat the sides completely; pour any excess chocolate back into the bowl. Set the half-moulds, open side down, on the prepared baking sheet and leave for 1–2 minutes until just set.

2 Apply a second coat of chocolate and chill for 1–3 minutes more, until set. Repeat a third time, then replace the moulds on the baking sheet and chill for at least 1 hour or until the chocolate has set completely. (Work quickly to avoid having to temper the chocolate again; untempered chocolate can be reheated if it hardens.)

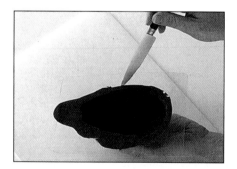

3 To remove the set chocolate, place a half-mould, open side up, on a board. Carefully trim any drops of chocolate from the edge of the mould. Gently insert the point of a small knife between the chocolate and the mould to break the air lock. Repeat with the second mould.

4 Holding the mould open side down, squeeze firmly to release the egg half. Repeat with the other half and chill, loosely covered. (Do not touch the chocolate surface with your fingers, as they will leave prints.) Reserve any melted chocolate to reheat for "glue".

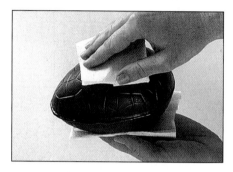

5 To assemble the egg, hold one half of the egg with a piece of folded kitchen paper or foil and fill with small truffles. If necessary, use the remaining melted chocolate as "glue". Spread a small amount on to the rim of the egg half and, holding the empty egg half with a piece of kitchen paper or foil, press it on to the filled half, making sure the rims are aligned and carefully joined.

6 Hold for several seconds, then prop up the egg with the folded paper or foil and chill to set. If you like, decorate the egg with ribbons or Easter decorations.

INDEX